BEAUTY AND

Praise for the series:

It was only a matter of time before a clever publisher realized that there is an audience for whom *Exile on Main Street* or *Electric Ladyland* are as significant and worthy of study as *The Catcher in the Rye* or *Middlemarch*. . . . The series . . . is freewheeling and eclectic, ranging from minute rock-geek analysis to idiosyncratic personal celebration—*The New York Times Book Review*

Ideal for the rock geek who thinks liner notes just aren't enough—*Rolling Stone*

One of the coolest publishing imprints on the planet—*Bookslut*

These are for the insane collectors out there who appreciate fantastic design, well-executed thinking, and things that make your house look cool. Each volume in this series takes a seminal album and breaks it down in startling minutiae. We love these. We are huge nerds—*Vice*

A brilliant series . . . each one a work of real love—*NME* (UK)

Passionate, obsessive, and smart—*Nylon*

Religious tracts for the rock 'n' roll faithful—*Boldtype*

[A] consistently excellent series—*Uncut* (UK)

We . . . aren't naive enough to think that we're your only source for reading about music (but if we had our way … watch out). For those of you who really like to know everything there is to know about an album, you'd do well to check out Bloomsbury's "33 1/3" series of books—*Pitchfork*

For almost 20 years, the 33-and-a-Third series of music books has focused on individual albums by acts well known (Bob Dylan, Nirvana, Abba, Radiohead), cultish (Neutral Milk Hotel, Throbbing Gristle, Wire) and many levels in-between. The range of music and their creators defines "eclectic," while the writing veers from freewheeling to acutely insightful. In essence, the books are for the music fan who (as Rolling Stone noted) "thinks liner notes just aren't enough."—*The Irish Times*

For reviews of individual titles in the series, please visit our blog at 333sound.com and our website at https://www.bloomsbury.com/academic/music-sound-studies/

Follow us on Twitter: @333books

Like us on Facebook: https://www.facebook.com/33.3books

For a complete list of books in this series, see the back of this book.

Forthcoming in the series:

and many more. . .

Beauty and the Beat

33⅓

Lisa Whittington-Hill

BLOOMSBURY ACADEMIC
NEW YORK • LONDON • OXFORD • NEW DELHI • SYDNEY

BLOOMSBURY ACADEMIC
Bloomsbury Publishing Inc
1385 Broadway, New York, NY 10018, USA
50 Bedford Square, London, WC1B 3DP, UK
29 Earlsfort Terrace, Dublin 2, Ireland

BLOOMSBURY, BLOOMSBURY ACADEMIC and the Diana logo are trade-marks of Bloomsbury Publishing Plc

First published in the United States of America 2023

Copyright © Lisa Whittington-Hill, 2023

For legal purposes the Acknowledgments on p. 101 constitute an extension of this copyright page.

All rights reserved. No part of this publication may be reproduced or transmit-ted in any form or by any means, electronic or mechanical, including photo-copying, recording, or any information storage or retrieval system, without prior permission in writing from the publishers.

Bloomsbury Publishing Inc does not have any control over, or responsibility for, any third-party websites referred to or in this book. All internet addresses given in this book were correct at the time of going to press. The author and publisher regret any inconvenience caused if addresses have changed or sites have ceased to exist, but can accept no responsibility for any such changes.

Whilst every effort has been made to locate copyright holders the publishers would be grateful to hear from any person(s) not here acknowledged.

A catalog record for this book is available from the Library of Congress.

ISBN: PB: 978-1-5013-9028-9
ePDF: 978-1-5013-9030-2
eBook: 978-1-5013-9029-6

Series: 33 ⅓

Typeset by Deanta Global Publishing Services, Chennai, India
Printed and bound in Great Britain

To find out more about our authors and books visit www.bloomsbury.com
and sign up for our newsletters.

Contents

Track Listing

1. "Our Lips Are Sealed" (2:45)
2. "How Much More" (3:06)
3. "Tonite" (3.35)
4. "Lust to Love" (4:04)
5. "This Town" (3:20)
6. "We Got the Beat" (2:36)
7. "Fading Fast" (3:41)
8. "Automatic" (3:07)
9. "You Can't Walk in Your Sleep (If You Can't Sleep)" (2:54)
10. "Skidmarks on My Heart" (3:06)
11. "Can't Stop the World" (3.20)

Introduction
Good Girls and Go-Go's

The Go-Go's debut album *Beauty and the Beat* was released the summer before my tenth birthday. I didn't immediately discover the album or the band. I was too preoccupied with trying to decide whether my upcoming birthday party should feature a My Pretty Pony or Strawberry Shortcake theme. Music at the time was Air Supply, REO Speedwagon, and "Jessie's Girl" by Rick Springfield. There was no MTV— although it would soon arrive—and my friends and I were still too young to really enjoy teen magazines like *Teen Beat* and *Tiger Beat*. For us, the idea of women and music was limited to Sheena Easton, Juice Newton, and Kim Carnes. All the records in my Mom's collection featured male singers like Barry Manilow, Engelbert Humperdinck, and Liberace. Please note that my Mom is hipper than this list makes her sound. An all-girl band that played instruments and wrote their own songs was something that didn't exist in our pre-teen world. That would soon change.

One of my friends had a sister who introduced us to the Go-Go's. We treated the band like cool older sisters who sang catchy songs and lived in some far-off, magical universe where Barry Manilow, math homework, and the flexed arm hang in gym class didn't exist. When I found out the Go-Go's were from Los Angeles, I spent my lunch hour in the school library figuring out where the city was in an atlas. It seemed so far from my home in Canada, even though it was only a four-hour plane ride away. When my Mom took me to California a couple of years later, I spent my time mainlining MTV, which was not yet available in Canada, and obsessively looking out the window of our rental car for one of the Go-Go's as if Kathy or Belinda would just be walking down the Ventura Freeway in the middle of a Wednesday afternoon.

Once we discovered *Beauty and the Beat*, it became the soundtrack to after-school hangouts and overnight sleepover parties. We would stay up well past our bedtimes, listening to "We Got the Beat" and recreating *Beauty and the Beat*'s iconic cover, which featured the band's five members in nothing but thick layers of face cream and white bath towels. We spent hours riding our ten-speed bikes around the neighborhood while drinking Slurpees and singing "This Town" at the top of our lungs. In our minds, we owned the town just like the Go-Go's did, even if our town was just the three-block radius around the local Red Rooster convenience store. When it was my turn to host the weekend sleepover, I pooled my allowance money together to get white towels that matched those on the album's cover. Using a Flintstones beach towel just didn't seem very Go-Go's. I should have just bought the towels at a department store, insisted my friends not wipe their messy, sleepover snack-covered hands on them, and then returned them for a refund just like the Go-Go's did for the album photo shoot.

The more we learned about the Go-Go's, or more accurately about the squeaky-clean image of the band that was marketed to us, the more we wanted to be just like them. When it was time for our school's annual talent show, featuring a lip-synch battle of the bands, my friends and I decided we wanted to be the Go-Go's and perform "Vacation" from the band's second album *Vacation*. It felt good to finally have an all-girl band to choose from. There was never a shortage of options for the boys, which made the inclusion of two dueling Van Halen bands confusing. Belinda, Jane, Charlotte, Kathy, and Gina made us feel like we could own the stage, that we belonged there and that we could beat not one but both Van Halens. My best friend Cara and I both wanted to be lead singer Belinda Carlisle for the show. Cara was blonde with a bouncy ponytail and blue eyes. She wore tight, striped polo shirts in pastel colors and always smelled like Love's Baby Soft cologne mist. When she stood in front of the Slurpee machine at the Red Rooster after school in her Jordache jeans, all the boys in our class stopped caring about the local hockey team and only cared about Cara. It was clear Cara was our Belinda. It was decided that I would play guitarist Jane Wiedlin, which I wasn't too happy about. Years later, I learned that being Jane, the original manic pixie dream girl, was cool. I also learned a lot more about my beloved childhood band. Perhaps, more than I was supposed to know.

* * *

The Go-Go's were marketed as America's sweethearts. In their first *Rolling Stone* cover story in 1982, their girl-next-door goodness was on full display. The band was described as "safe, wholesome and proudly commercial."[1] The magazine called them "heroes for the little sisters of the longhaired guys who play air guitar at Foreigner concerts,"[2] and as evidenced by YouTube clips of concerts from the band's 1982 tour, which show an audience of screaming teen and pre-teen girls, the magazine was right. Cara and her Jordaches would have fit right in.

What didn't quite fit was the disconnect between how the band was marketed and who the Go-Go's really were. "We were cute and bubbly, but we were also twisted, crazy, drug-addict sex fiends,"[3] said Wiedlin in an interview in the *Behind the Music* episode devoted to the Go-Go's. We all knew they were cute and bubbly, the twisted part, well, not so much. We also didn't know much about the band's punk past and roots in the 1970s Los Angeles punk scene. If the Go-Go's had seemed foreign to Cara and me, just imagine what bands like the Bags or the Germs would have done to our fragile, sheltered pre-teen brains. The band's punk past was not a part of the packaging of the Go-Go's that was pushed on young fans, record buyers, and the press. In the days before the internet, social media, and TMZ, it was easier to control and craft a band's image and stay on message. "If it wasn't for the punk rock scene, the Go-Go's never would've happened. Bottom line,"[4] said Carlisle in a 2020 *Vogue* oral history devoted to *Beauty and the Beat*. Pre-Go-Go's Carlisle almost became a member of the influential Los Angeles punk band the Germs as drummer Dottie Danger, but a case of mono kept her from fully committing.

When the Go-Go's signed to Miles Copeland's I.R.S. Records in April 1981, after being turned down by countless record companies because they were girls, their initial punk sound was given a pop polish. This was something the band rebelled against both while recording their debut album and when they heard the final product. "When the mix of *Beauty and the Beat* was sent to us, we all went out to the car to listen to it on the stereo—and we were *horrified*. We were so disappointed that it sounded the way it did. We wanted it to be faster and raunchier,"[5] Carlisle told NPR in 2020 of the band's initial reaction to the record. While the album may have featured a more pop sound, part of the band's success, and appeal, was their ability to bridge pop and punk music.

When it came to their past, the Go-Go's lips really were sealed. The group's wholesome image masked the hard partying, heroin and cocaine, all things we glorify when it comes to male musicians but criticize, mock, and constantly make women apologize for. All-male bands like Mötley Crüe and Guns N' Roses are treated like heroes for their hard-partying ways and tales of their drinking, drugs, and sex with groupies are well documented. Female musicians are not allowed to, or expected to, party as hard as their male counterparts.

When I later learned about the Go-Go's partying, drug, and alcohol use and less than wholesome image, I felt betrayed. (Fun fact: one band member was kicked out of Ozzy Osbourne's hotel room for partying too hard.) What happened to my wholesome sleepover idols? The Go-Go's were a game-changing band for me growing up and they had lied to me. I wondered if Cara knew. Of course, the Go-Go's hadn't deceived me; the music industry, media, and society were to blame. For the band to be accepted and be popular, there were, unfortunately, parts of themselves they had to keep hidden.

"There was a real desire on the part of the media and society for us to be nonthreatening and wholesome . . . We could have done more to try to control the way our image was thrust on us, but for some reason, that had to be part of the package in order for us to be accepted,"[6] said bassist Kathy Valentine in the book *We Gotta Get Out of This Place: The True, Tough Story of Women in Rock*. When the band tried to control their image, they were often powerless in the face of the misogyny of the music industry. When the Go-Go's appeared on the cover of *Rolling Stone* for the first time in 1982, they wanted to avoid an overly sexual image. The cover featured the Go-Go's in underwear—but unsexy, plain, white, men's Hanes underwear. The image may have been wholesome, but *Rolling Stone* ran it with a coverline that said, "Go-Go's Put Out." When the band's manager Ginger Canzoneri called *Rolling Stone* publisher Jann Wenner to complain about the sexist cover, he implied the band should have been grateful to be on the cover at all. Magazines like *Rolling Stone* love to market female artists as good girls but then turn around and exploit their sexuality to sell copies.

*   *   *

Beauty and the Beat was the first, and to date only, album to reach the number one spot by an all-girl group who not only wrote their own songs but also played their own instruments. The critically acclaimed album spent six weeks at the top of the *Billboard* charts in March 1982 and has sold over two million copies, making it one of the most successful debut albums of all time. The album featured two Top 100 hit singles: "We Got the Beat," which went to number two on the charts, and "Our Lips Are Sealed," which landed at number twenty. It also earned the band a Grammy nomination in 1982 for Best New Artist. They lost to Sheena Easton. Despite their success, the Go-Go's were manufactured and marketed by the press and the music industry as good girls to sell their records. Their accomplishments and talent were often ignored at the expense of a focus on their looks and love lives. They were treated as a novelty act and had their story rewritten to sell records.

Years have passed since the Go-Go's were head over heals, but, sadly, the gender bias that greeted the band and *Beauty and the Beat* continues today. Female musicians are still pigeonholed into tired and outdated sexist stereotypes. The marketing of the good girl image that was so popular with the Go-Go's still exists and has been used to sell everyone from Britney Spears to Selena Gomez. Bad girls in music may exist, but only so they can be pitted against the good girl with media-manufactured feuds and competition— think early 2000-era Britney and Christina. *Beauty and the Beat* meant an image makeover for the Go-Go's as they went from punk to pop. Carefully constructed and controlled image makeovers have become the standard now for pop princesses. There's a script that must be adhered to and considerable damage control and spin happens when female musicians go off script or simply mature and outgrow it.

To talk about *Beauty and the Beat* is to talk about the contradictions that existed with the Go-Go's and the image of the band that was marketed. It also means acknowledging that although the Go-Go's broke barriers, media, society, and the music industry still treat female musicians in the same way they did when *Beauty and the Beat* was released.

*   *   *

The Go-Go's, a new documentary about the band by director Alison Ellwood, premiered at Sundance in 2020 to rave reviews. That same year, the band released "Club Zero," their first new music in nineteen years, and announced a reunion tour. And it wasn't just the Go-Go's that were in the news again. The female musicians they helped paved the way for, and that endured the same sexist treatment the Go-Go's experienced, were too. From Bikini Kill touring again to *Framing Britney Spears*, the 2021 documentary that reignited the debate around Spears' conservatorship and how the singer was treated by the press, to the controversy over a very glammed-up Billie Eilish on the cover of *Vogue*. Pop, and not so pop in Bikini Kill's case, princesses were big again.

While writing the proposal for this book, my Twitter feed exploded with the news that the Go-Go's would finally be inducted into the Rock & Roll Hall of Fame. The class of inductees included two women (Tina Turner and Carole King) which, sadly, is considered groundbreaking. There were also two bands being inducted that included former members of the Germs (Pat Smear of Foo Fighters and Carlisle), which is a nice nod to the Go-Go's punk past. Many assumed the Go-Go's were already in the Hall of Fame. At the end of Ellwood's documentary Police drummer Stewart Copeland comments, "What the fuck? They're not?"[7] echoing the sentiments of many.

But it is not just the Hall of Fame that excluded the Go-Go's. They are often left out of the narrative when it comes to feminist bands and influential female artists. The Go-Go's played their own instruments and wrote their own songs. They had a female manager, which was not the norm at the time. They also had female roadies, which was unheard of in 1981. They partied as hard as their male counterparts and made no excuses for their ambition or the evolution of their sound. They weren't the fun-loving, wholesome singing girl gang who all got along, and they never made apologies for that. One of the greatest and most successful all-girl groups in music history, the Go-Go's influence on female musicians has often been downplayed. They were trailblazers and no album by the band exemplifies this spirit more than *Beauty and the Beat*. The Go-Go's embraced the DIY spirit of riot grrrl before there was a Bikini Kill or a Bratmobile. "From the beginning our motto has been: 'Do what you don't know how to do,'"[8] Wiedlin said in a 1982 interview.

They were brash and unapologetic long before Courtney Love. Girls making music on their own terms didn't start with Taylor Swift or Beyoncé; it started with the Go-Go's. A girl power anthem like the Spice Girls' "Wannabe" would not exist without the punk power anthem "We Got the Beat." The Go-Go's were a feminist band, but they aren't regarded as one. They were the original girls with guitars and attitude, and *Beauty and the Beat* was a feminist album, long before making an empowering call to arms was considered cool. *Beauty and the Beat* inspired me to pick up an air guitar when I was younger and still inspires me to make music, to make art, and to do it on my own terms. There are countless girls like me who count the Go-Go's as influences from musicians like Haim and Kathleen Hanna to actress Drew Barrymore to comedian Margaret Cho.

Beauty and the Beat turned forty in 2021. Let's celebrate the legendary album, let's celebrate the groundbreaking band, and let's finally give the Go-Go's their feminist due. Like my Mom abandoning her Barry Manilow records, it's about time.

1
Like the Buzzcocks, but Women

The Go-Go's roots lay firmly in punk rock, specifically the Los Angeles punk rock scene in the mid-to-late 1970s. "There never would have been the Go-Go's without the punk rock scene in Los Angeles,"[1] Jane Wiedlin admitted early in *The Go-Go's*, Alison Ellwood's documentary about the band. A small, close-knit community, which supported musical experimentation, freedom of expression, and collaboration, the city's punk scene included bands from the Weirdos and the Germs to X and the Zeros. It was a diverse scene where everyone was welcome. There were few rules and even fewer barriers between the audience and the bands.

"The 1970s Hollywood punk scene was a space where I could be with other, like-minded individuals who also felt disenfranchised or alienated by the communities where we had grown up: our schools, our families, our neighborhoods,"[2] said Alice Bag, lead singer of the Los Angeles punk band the Bags, in a 2014 *Razorcake* oral history of the city's first wave of punk. Often overshadowed by London's punk scene, which was driven by politics and class struggle, or New York punk, a darker, more art-focused scene, the Los Angeles scene included, and encouraged, women making music. There was Bag and her bandmate Pat Bag, Lorna Doom, bassist for the Germs, and X's Exene Cervenka. In 1978, there would be another group of women to add to this list when Wiedlin, Belinda Carlisle, and Margot Olavarria formed a new all-girl group called the Go-Go's.

Carlisle and Wiedlin, known then as Jane Drano, lived across the courtyard from each other at the Canterbury, a 1920s apartment building on Cherokee Avenue in Hollywood, which served as a roach-infested ground zero for the city's punk scene and was even the inspiration for one of the Go-Go's first songs ("Living at the Canterbury" written by Wiedlin). Along with Olavarria, they attended punk shows at venues like the Masque, located in the basement of the Pussycat porno theater and conveniently only a block from the Canterbury, Starwood, and Whisky a Go-Go seeing local bands like the Screamers and the Dickies and touring acts that included Devo, Blondie, and the Ramones. Carlisle, Wiedlin, and Olavarria felt like the only members of their small punk community who weren't playing in a band and decided that needed to change. Their final inspiration would come from a trip to San Francisco in January 1978 to see the Sex Pistols play at the Winterland Ballroom in what would be the band's final show. Discussing the show later at a house party, the three decided it was time to finally start a band. "We sealed the deal by telling each other that at the least we could be as bad as everyone else, but the unique thing that happened and separated us from the pack from the start was that we also agreed that we didn't *have* to be bad,"[3] Carlisle wrote in *Lips Unsealed*, her 2010 memoir.

"I think the reason I ended up getting in this band is because everyone we knew and everyone we hung out with were all in a band and *they* weren't any good—we knew they weren't great musicians—so we figured if they could do it, why couldn't we?"[4] said Wiedlin in a 1980 *Sounds* interview. There was just one problem with their plan. They didn't know how to play any instruments. Embracing the scene's DIY ethos, they refused to let a lack of musical skills stop them and started to learn how to play.

"It was DIY and if you were terrible, you were cooler, and anybody could do whatever they wanted. It was total freedom,"[5] said Carlisle in Ellwood's doc of the scene's early days. It was decided that she would be the singer, Olavarria would play bass and Wiedlin guitar, in addition to backing vocals. The band's original lineup also included Elissa Bello, the cousin of a high school friend of Olavarria's, on drums. "I wanted to throw up on stage, rip my clothes off, and dye my hair,"[6] Wiedlin told *Flipside* in 1979 of the band's formation, while Olavarria just wanted to "spit at Valley girls,"[7] ironic since Wiedlin and Carlisle were both from the Valley. Carlisle had been a popular cheerleader in high school whose life was changed the first time she heard *Raw Power* by the Stooges. Wiedlin was studying fashion design at Los Angeles Trade Tech prior to the Go-Go's. She was fascinated by the punk fashion she saw in the pages of UK magazines, but soon discovered there was an actual punk scene happening closer to home in Los Angeles.

The Go-Go's played their first show, an unofficial, hastily organized set opening for local band the Dickies at the

Masque in May 1978. They didn't need to write their set list down since it included only three songs, one of which they played twice. This was all the material the band had at the time. "Even though they were just starting to play, you could tell they had songwriting ability . . . People remembered their clever lyrics, that they had cool melodies. They had something special even at that first show,"[8] Bag, who attended the Masque show, told NPR in a 2020 oral history of *Beauty and the Beat*. Carlisle's memories of the show weren't as positive. "I remember people were either laughing hysterically or looked absolutely mortified,"[9] she told *Behind the Music*. One early review of the band remarked: "The Go-Go's are to music what botulism is to tuna."[10] When it came time to name the new band, they narrowed it down to two possibilities, the Go-Go's or the Misfits. When the Kinks released *Misfits* in 1978, the band scrapped that name over fears people would think they had stolen it. *Webster's Dictionary* defined "go-go" as "joyous, carefree and fun," which seemed like a perfect fit for the band, so they christened themselves the Go-Go's.

Early on the band decided there was something or someone missing. The Go-Go's needed a band member, who knew about music and could play an instrument or, at the very least, knew how to turn on an amp. Charlotte Caffey was playing bass in the local band the Eyes in April 1978 when Olavarria and Carlisle approached her backstage at the Starwood about playing guitar in their new girl group. The Eyes had just opened for the Jam and Caffey remembers Carlisle was wearing a trash bag cinched at the waist as a dress and ripped fishnet stockings and had purple hair.

Caffey accepted their invitation even though she played bass, not guitar. In true Go-Go's DIY spirit, Caffey learned to play guitar and joined the Go-Go's.

"First of all she was a real musician; she'd gone to musical college, studied piano, she knew how to read music, all this stuff that we didn't know how to do. But she also brought with her a pop sensibility she wasn't afraid to show,"[11] Wiedlin said of Caffey's influence on the band. With their lineup now in place and the band getting better, the Go-Go's played their first official show at The Rock Corporation in August 1978. A review in *Slash*, a punk rock fanzine, was positive, calling the Go-Go's "a new fun group"[12] and "a dynamic set of female rockers."[13] The band was busy rehearsing, writing, and playing shows, but not everyone could commit to being a Go-Go full time. Bello was replaced in 1979 by Gina Schock, a drummer from Baltimore who had played in the band Edie and the Eggs, with John Waters film star Edith Massey. Not only was Schock an experienced drummer, but she also bought a discipline and work ethic to the band that had been missing. She encouraged them to practice more often, and they encouraged her to ditch her overalls and frizzy permed hair in favor of a punk rock makeover.

In December 1979, while playing as the house band at the Whisky, the Go-Go's opened for the English ska band Madness. This led to an invitation for the Go-Go's to open for Madness and the Specials on a UK tour in the spring. The Go-Go's quit their jobs and sold their stuff to finance the trip which they were convinced was going to make them stars. In addition to superstardom, the Go-Go's hoped the tour would lead to a recording contract. The tour didn't quite go as planned. Both Madness and the Specials attracted members of the far-right National Front to their shows. An all-girl group from California didn't win over the crowds who spit at the band, threw bottles, and greeted the Go-Go's with "show us your tits." The band often left the stage crying, with Carlisle covered in spit. Madness and the Specials proved to be more welcoming to the Go-Go's than their audiences, which was a source of comfort, and romance, as the tour dragged on. The Go-Go's hid their disappointment over the tour, writing to friends and family back home they told them how well it was going and how popular they were with UK audiences.

While in the UK, Go-Go's manager Ginger Canzoneri shopped around the band's demo that included an early recording of "We Got the Beat," a song Caffey wrote.

> I was spending New Year's Day [1980] alone, listening to Motown songs, watching a *Twilight Zone* marathon and getting high on a cocktail of stuff. All day I was trying to write a song. I stopped and said, "F—it, I don't care." The minute I did that, boom, an idea popped into my head. I ran to get my cassette recorder and sang "We Got the Beat" into the recorder to document it. I knew I had written something special. It took two minutes. I didn't labor on the lyrics. It's a simple song, which goes back to the '60s, when I had my ears glued to the radio for the Stones, the Beatles, and the Beach Boys.[14]

Canzoneri eventually negotiated a one single deal with Stiff Records, a UK label that was home to Madness, and "We Got the Beat" was released as an import single in the United

States, where it became a minor club hit. The Go-Go's flew back to Los Angeles and did nothing to dispel the growing rumors that they were big in Europe. Upon their return, they played at the Starwood and the line for the show was around the block. The band was also surprised to see that it wasn't just their usual punk audience and friends that were there to see them play. But not everyone was happy with the band's success. Olavarria objected to the packaging of the band and the more accessible pop direction their sound was taking. The band had shows booked at the Whisky over New Year's 1980 when Olavarria got sick and couldn't play. They needed to find someone who could replace her for the shows. Kathy Valentine was catching a show at the Whisky on Christmas night when Caffey approached her in the bathroom and asked if she could fill in on bass for the upcoming Whisky shows. Valentine had played in the Los Angeles band the Textones but was a guitarist and not a bassist. She had initially seen the Go-Go's play with the local band the Plugz and wasn't impressed, but after seeing them play a show with Schock, she saw how far they had come musically. "I caught them again at the Starwood one night. They wore lots of colours and stripes and bounced around energetically, but what I really noticed was how the audience went nuts for them,"[15] Valentine wrote in her 2020 memoir *All I Ever Wanted*. She spent three days learning the band's material and the bass with the aid of a rehearsal tape and a bunch of cocaine. She played her first show with the band on New Year's Eve and after the Whisky gigs were up, she wanted to stay. The other band members wanted her to, as well.

"You couldn't deny the fact we were a better band with Kathy—so what are you going to do?"[16] Carlisle told *Smash Hits* magazine in 1982. Olavarria was let go from the Go-Go's. Some members of the punk scene objected to her firing and accused the Go-Go's of selling out. They didn't want the band's sound or image to evolve beyond their punk beginnings. While the Go-Go's roots may have been in punk, their future lay in pop. "We all had pop sensibilities. The Buzzcocks is probably the one band we all loved. We were a punk band, but as we became more adept with our instruments, we were a pop band,"[17] said Carlisle. Critics were also skeptical of the Go-Go's. Writing in *New York Rocker* in 1980 Don Snowden said:

> It wasn't so much the lack of musical competence or the trendy posing that put me off the Go-Go's initially as the aftermath of their first few performances . . . It looked like nothing more than another LA triumph of style over substance, a punkette variation of Kim Fowley's oh-so-tired "teen dream jailbait playing rock 'n' roll hustle."[18]

New York Rocker even awarded the Go-Go's the Shock of the Month Award for being "an alarmingly good *real* band as opposed to an *all-girl band*."[19] Apparently, for *New York Rocker,* and sadly many other critics, the two were mutually exclusive. In their early days and throughout their career, people assumed the Go-Go's were manufactured, put together by Fowley or some other puppeteer Svengali. They assumed their songs had been written by someone else, usually a man, and that the band didn't actually play any instruments. But the Go-Go's did it all themselves. They wrote their own music and played their own instruments. The Go-Go's not only had autonomy but also had ambition believing they could be as good, if not better, than the boys. Girls having ambition and autonomy? For male critics like Snowden, it's unthinkable, a shock that lasts much longer than a month. If they're good and if they're girls, there must be a man behind it.

"I'm very serious about wanting people to think of the Go-Go's as a band that is musically good, not just a 'girl' band,"[20] said Carlisle in an interview in *Slash*. The zine was an early champion of the Go-Go's, but resented the band when it adopted a more mainstream approach and sound. "What happened was that we improved musically, and a lot of people had thought we were something we weren't. They began to hear that we had harmonies, which were failed efforts before, and that we were really trying on the musical part,"[21] said Caffey in *New York Rocker*. Early in the history of the Go-Go's, critics often fixated on how the band couldn't play their instruments, something that was regarded as a badge of honor and a sign of authenticity for male musicians in the DIY punk scene. Early show reviews talked about how the Go-Go's were growing stronger as a band, learning to play their instruments and write songs. In the press, there was an emphasis on the band's progress and a focus on how "good" the band was becoming, but a definition of "good" that was usually measured by some male music journalist. Then there's a shift when the band becomes too good and they're labeled sellouts, manufactured, too ambitious. "For the first few years when we were just learning how to play, I think we sounded probably a lot worse than we meant to, just because we didn't know what we were doing. And then slowly, as we learned to play, the songs started coming out more and more,"[22] Wiedlin told *Songfacts* in 2007.

It was not only critics and journalists who treated the band like a novelty act. For record labels, the idea of five girls playing music together had about as much weight as Carlisle's old trash bag dresses. After the success of the Stiff Records single, the Go-Go's wanted a record deal. Not surprisingly, like critics and journalists, record labels were also skeptical. No label would sign the band and Canzoneri had a folder full of rejections. Record execs didn't think an all-girl group could sell records. "Good luck with your enterprising girl group,"[23] read one rejection letter. Canzoneri told *Trouser Press* in 1981:

> [I]t took about a full year of hard work to get this band signed. The one thing I was greeted with without exception from every company was, "Oh, it's an all girl band. Fanny didn't make it, the Runaways didn't make it, therefore girl bands don't make it. No thank you; I think it's interesting, but it's not right for us."[24]

"We were told, 'We love you. We can see that everybody loves you, but there's never been an all-female band that has been big,'"[25] said Carlisle in 2020.

"Why Can't the Go-Go's Get a Record Deal?" asked the headline of a *Los Angeles Times* piece that discussed other less popular bands than the Go-Go's who had been signed. The answer was "sexism," but it took the writer a much longer word count to arrive at this answer. Had the Go-Go's been men, they would never have faced the challenges they did in securing a record deal. "It was either that we were girls so they didn't want to take a chance, or we were girls and they wanted to capitalize on that,"[26] explained Wiedlin in a 1981 issue of *Trouser Press*. Eventually, the Go-Go's signed to I.R.S. Records, a label Miles Copeland had started, which was home to bands like the Buzzcocks, who the Go-Go's loved and hoped their band would emulate, the Cramps, and Oingo Boingo. Copeland said in NPR's *Beauty and the Beat* oral history:

> The Go-Go's and the Bangles and the other girl groups were turned down because they were all girls. Labels would say, "Well, a girl group would never happen, do we want to take the risk and sign you? No." I don't think the people actually listened to the music or went to the shows to see the excitement of the audience.[27]

Copeland not only listened to the music but also believed in the Go-Go's. The *Los Angeles Times* could rest easy. The Go-Go's finally had a record deal.

2
Good Luck Enterprising Girl Groups

When the Go-Go's formed in May 1978, the idea of an all-girl group that not only wrote their own songs but played their own instruments was largely unheard of. Women could be vocalists in girl groups like the Supremes or the Crystals, but the songs they sang were written by men. Sometimes men did more than just write the songs, in the case of all-female bands like the Runaways and the Ronettes who had controlling men pulling the strings, and calling the shots behind the scenes. Bands that weren't controlled by a man and featured women playing instruments, like Fanny and the Raincoats, sadly, never achieved the level of commercial success or sold as many records as the Go-Go's did. To see how the Go-Go's changed not only the musical landscape but the idea of what a female musician could accomplish, it's important to look at the girl groups that came before.

The Shirelles were the first all-female group to have a number one single with "Will You Love Me Tomorrow," which was released in 1960. The group is credited with launching the popular girl group era of the early to mid-

1960s. "The importance of the girl group image and its effect on the female rock audience has traditionally been overlooked by rock historians, who tend to regard girl groups as interchangeable, easily manipulated puppets, while the ones with the 'real' talent were the managers, songwriters, publishers, and producers who worked behind the groups,"[1] wrote Gillian G. Gaar in *She's a Rebel: The History of Women in Rock & Roll*, describing the girl groups of the 1960s. That "real" talent belonged to those who wrote the songs and in the case of many 1960s girl groups that was a man or a team of men. Women were just the vocalists, which led to them being easily dismissed and treated as disposable. "Once a winning formula for a group had been identified, it was repeated in subsequent singles until the group stopped having hits. The group was then left to return to obscurity, while the production teams moved on to the next formula and the next group,"[2] said Gaar.

One of the 1960s girl groups the Go-Go's has named as an inspiration was the Shangri-Las. They have even covered the band's 1964 song "Remember (Walking in the Sand)" in live performances. If you're not familiar with that song, you might be familiar with the Shangri-Las number one song "Leader of the Pack," which was released in 1965. The Go-Go's were often compared to 1960s bands like the Shangri-Las. This was not necessarily because the two bands sounded or looked alike. Journalists consistently grouped female bands together, which not only gave the impression of a monolithic group but also treated women like a musical genre. Female bands were rarely compared to other male musicians. They were always measured against, and mentioned with, other women. "The Go-Go's are inheriting the mantle of the 60s great girl groups. There's no copycat style going on just five people who love this kind of music and know what they want. They've cut their teeth on the school of Shangri-Las, Ronettes, Crystals, and even the Supremes, then thrown it out for a completely different approach,"[3] read a review of the "We've Got the Beat/How Much More" Stiff Records import single in *Slash*.

The Go-Go's weren't controlled by a man, which is one of the things that set them apart from other bands that came before. It was a source of pride for the Go-Go's that they did it themselves. "[T]here was usually a seedy, cigar-chompin' guy lurking just behind the curtain, pulling strings, writing songs and shaping the image as his gals danced on his string. But The Go-Go's didn't need a doctor in their house."[4] One of the most famous of these doctors was Kim Fowley, the Svengali behind the Los Angeles group the Runaways. The band formed a few years before the Go-Go's in 1975. Guitarist Joan Jett and drummer Sandy West were teenagers when they were introduced to each other by local producer, promoter, and musician Fowley who helped them recruit the band's other members. Lita Ford joined the Runaways on lead guitar, Jackie Fox on bass, and Cherie Currie as singer. The Runaways had first added singer/bassist Micki (Michael) Steele, who was fired but would go on to join another all-female band, the Bangles. Fowley not only produced and co-wrote songs for the Runaways but was also their manager. "While the girls yearned to be taken seriously as musicians, Fowley insisted on selling them as hard-rock jailbait. He played up the youth angle every chance he got, recognizing that rebellious young women were craving self-expression and that male audiences found bad-girl fantasies appealing,"[5] wrote Jason Cherkis in "The Lost Girls," his 2015 *Huffington Post* investigative piece on the Runaways and Fowley. On the back of the band's first album, Fowley had each girl's age next to their photo. Fowley's jailbait marketing strategy, while utterly disgusting, resonated with the sexist music industry and media. From headlines like "The Sex Kittens of Rock"[6] and "Teenaged, Wild & Braless"[7] to a *Crawdaddy* cover story that featured the author talking about how after witnessing Currie sing "Cherry Bomb," he was "overcome with the urge to jack off against the stage."[8] Charming.

The Runaways signed to Mercury Records, released their debut album *The Runaways* in 1976, and then toured the United States supporting bands like Cheap Trick and Talking Heads. Currie wrote in her memoir *Neon Angel*:

> We were young and pissed off, and wanted everything right now, now, now! And the music reflected that. Our songs were about drinking, boys, staying out late, screaming "fuck authority." It may have been rough around the edges, but it had a certain kind of teenage energy that you can't fake. Even though the band started off as concept, we quickly became a real band.[9]

The Runaways second album *Queens of Noise* and a US tour followed in 1977, as well as a tour of Japan where they recorded *Live in Japan*. Fowley and the Runaways parted ways in 1977 and the group split in 1979, but by that point both Currie and Fox had already left. Fowley died of bladder cancer in 2015 and after his death Fox came forward to say Fowley had raped her. Fowley manipulated the band members, often pitting them against each other, and parents of the girls accused him of breaking promises when it came to schooling for the band members. "He dictated what the girls wore and how they moved on stage, going so far as to hire a choreographer—at the band's expense—to teach Currie how to whip a microphone around on a cord and sling it up between her legs from behind,"[10] wrote Cherkis in "Lost Girls."

*　*　*

Fanny formed in Los Angeles in 1969 and achieved success, but never at the level the band aspired to or deserved. The Go-Go's, the Bangles, and the Runaways have all listed Fanny as an influence. Fanny was the first all-female band to release an album on a major label, with their 1970 debut *Fanny*. "There were all-girl bands before us, but there was no other all-girl band that had been signed to a major label to release full albums. Goldie And The Gingerbreads, Isis and the Pleasure Seekers were around but they were only putting out singles,"[11] said Fanny drummer Alice de Buhr in a 2015 *Classic Rock* interview.

The band was started by sisters June and Jean Millington who grew up in Manila but moved to Sacramento, California, in 1961. They were the daughters of a Filipina mom and a US Navy officer dad. The sisters felt like outsiders in Sacramento and started playing music to make new friends. By 1965 they had formed the Svelts, their first band. Fanny was discovered while playing as Wild Honey at an unsigned music night at the Troubadour in Los Angeles. The band was signed to Reprise Records by producer Richard Perry in 1970 when he was looking for an all-girl band to mentor. In fact, they were signed before the label even heard them. Despite their actual musical talent, Reprise was just looking for a novelty act in the form of an all-girl band. The band's name was changed from Wild Honey to Fanny and the original band lineup included June on guitar, Jean on bass, de Buhr on drums, and Nickey Barclay on keyboards with the sisters and Barclay alternating lead vocals on various songs.

"Women who could rock hard were a rarity in those days," Jean told *Classic Rock*. "Most of the girl bands were novelty acts. When we were sixteen, seventeen years old and playing up in Reno, there was a band called Eight Of A Kind—four females who performed topless, you know what I mean? That's what we were up against."[12] The band's second album, *Charity Ball*, was released in 1971. Its title track reached number forty on the *Billboard* charts and Fanny toured the world, opening for Humble Pie and Jethro Tull. *Fanny Hill*, their third album, was released in 1972, and a fourth album *Mother's Pride*, produced by Todd Rundgren, followed in 1973. At this point, the record label wanted the band to adopt a sexier hard-rock image, including skimpier onstage outfits. "We were in front of a chalet and the photographer wanted us to get on our hands and knees, like submissive creatures. I turned to our road manager and said to him: 'Do we have to do this?' And he very quietly said: 'Yes,'"[13] June said of a Fanny photoshoot. "It felt like all our hard work was being chucked away for this crap idea that girls couldn't possibly be decent musicians."[14]

June resisted the sexier image the label wanted and increasingly felt constricted by the group. She quit in 1973. De Buhr also quit and a new lineup released the band's final album *Rock and Roll Survivors* in 1974. The first single "I've Had It" reached number seventy-nine on the *Billboard* charts and the second single, "Butter Boy," written by Jean, reached number twenty-nine. Unfortunately, they couldn't celebrate the success of "Butter Boy" because the band had split by that time. Fanny wanted to be judged on their musical skills and not their sex appeal. They focused on musical talent and developing a good live performance, which they felt was necessary to challenge audience assumptions that girls couldn't play instruments or weren't talented musicians. "We knew we had to prove we could play and deliver live. Otherwise, no one would believe it,"[15] June told *Vintage Guitar* magazine. Despite this, the first question the band was often asked in interviews was, "How does it feel to be a girl playing an instrument?" and headlines like "Fanny, a Four-Girl Rock Group, Poses a Challenge to Male Ego" and "Girl Rock Band Still Feminine" accompanied pieces about the band.

* * *

A history of female bands would be incomplete without acknowledging the female punk and post-punk bands in England that proceeded the Go-Go's. "The space provided within punk for the untrained to make music enabled post-punk women to overcome a lack of precedent in forming bands and taking non-vocal roles,"[16] Rhian E. Jones wrote in her chapter on post-punk in *Women Make Noise: Girl Bands from Motown to the Modern.* The Slits were an all-female punk band that formed in London in 1976 at a time when it was still uncommon to see women playing instruments or owning the stage. "We weren't following a band. We were the band,"[17] said guitarist Viv Albertine in the documentary *Here to Be Heard: The Story of the Slits.* The group's main lineup consisted of Ari Up (singer), Palmolive (drummer), Albertine, and Tessa Pollitt (bassist). "Here come the punkesses,"[18] announced the *News of the World* in a piece on the Slits, although the paper wouldn't print the band's actual name because they thought it was too vulgar. The Slits also hated being called things like "punkesses" and "punkettes."

"The Slits distinctively experimental sound—a slippery, loose and spacious dub-punk hybrid—stemmed partly from an absence of established rock 'n' roll references of the kind motivating their male contemporaries,"[19] wrote Jones in *Women Make Noise.* Their debut album *Cut* was released in 1979 on Island Records, a year after the Go-Go's formed, and was considered a defining post-punk album. "It unlocked something for me and suddenly I was standing there thinking 'Wow, I want to do this too,'"[20] Gina Birch, vocalist and bassist of the Raincoats, a UK all-female post-punk band, said of seeing the Slits for the first time. The Slits supported the Clash on their 1977 White Riot Tour, along with the Buzzcocks, and toured again with the Clash in November 1978. The bus driver on the White Riot Tour had to be bribed to let the Slits on the bus; he was threatened by the band and their presence. A hotel also refused to allow them to stay after seeing "The Slits" written on Pollitt's guitar case. "There was such hostility at that time because they were an intrusion. Women were supposed to know their place and their place was to be wearing clothes that some other bloke dictated, singing what some regular guy wanted them to sing,"[21] said journalist and *Revenge of the She-Punks* author Vivien Goldman in the Slits documentary.

Palmolive left the Slits in 1978 and joined the Raincoats. She was replaced by a male drummer, Budgie (Peter Clarke). The Slits released their second studio album, *Return of the Giant Slits*, in 1981 and toured widely before breaking up in 1982. Up and Pollitt reformed the Slits in 2005 with new members. In 2006, the band went on a US tour for the first time in twenty-five years, followed by tours of Australia and Japan. More lineup changes followed, and the band released their third album, *Trapped Animal*, in 2009. Sadly, Up died in October 2010 and the video for *Trapped Animal's* "Lazy Slam" was released following her death.

Bands like Fanny and the Shangri-Las not only inspired the Go-Go's, but also showed the band how they could forge a different path.

3
From Punk to Pop

The Go-Go's signed to Miles Copeland's label I.R.S. on April 1, 1981. It's fitting that the band would sign their record deal on April Fool's Day since for many record execs the idea of women playing music was nothing more than a joke. After signing their deal, the Go-Go's headed to New York City to record their debut album. Copeland hired Richard Gottehrer to produce the album. Gottehrer was a songwriter and producer who had success with songs like "Hang on Sloopy," "My Boyfriend's Back," and "I Want Candy" by the Strangeloves. Gottehrer also started Sire Records with Seymour Stein and the label had helped launch the careers of bands like Blondie and the Ramones, which appealed to the Go-Go's and their punk roots. Gottehrer had even produced Blondie's 1976 self-titled debut album.

Gottehrer wanted to polish the band's sound, slow down their songs so you could hear the lyrics, and make their music more accessible to a pop audience. "I told them they had to slow down, put the songs into a groove. The songs deserved to be treated with respect,"[1] Gottehrer told

Billboard in 2016. He had a small budget of $35,000 for the recording and ended up going over budget by $7,500, which he paid for out of his own pocket (not to worry, he later made it back in royalties). The Go-Go's didn't want to record a new version of "We Got the Beat" for the album. They argued they already had the Stiff Records version and people seemed to like it, but Gottehrer felt *Beauty and the Beat* needed a new recording of the song and finally convinced them. The album also included the hit single "Our Lips Are Sealed" for which Wiedlin wrote the lyrics and music. The song's lyrics were based on lines from a love letter sent to Wiedlin by Terry Hall from the Specials, as Wiedlin and Hall had been romantically involved, while the Specials and the Go-Go's were touring with Madness in the UK. Hall's band Fun Boy Three would also end up recording a version of the song.

While Gottehrer tried to slow down the band's songs, what he couldn't slow down was the Go-Go's partying. The girls made the most of their time in NYC, taking advantage of the city's nightlife and everything it had to offer. "This was when I learned that girls can be as disruptive and dirty as boys. Who knew? It might have been drinking, it might've been going out, looking for booty—I'm not sure if they were into their drug phase yet. But that energy and personality came across on the record,"[2] Gottehrer told *Billboard*. When the Go-Go's heard *Beauty and the Beat* for the first time they cried, but they weren't exactly tears of joy. They thought they were making a punk record and expected the record to sound like the band did live. Their punk sound had been given a pop polish by Gottehrer. "A couple of us were concerned about how our peers in L.A. perceived us. With the small amount of success we'd had, people said we sold out, we weren't punk after all, blah, blah, blah. Hearing the album made us feel like they were right—we sounded like we sold out,"[3] Carlisle told *Billboard* in 2016. The Go-Go's were not the only ones who were upset upon hearing the album. Copeland thought Gottehrer had ruined the band by delivering a pop album. Like the band, Copeland was under the misconception that Gottehrer was delivering a punk album. Later, when the album went to the number one spot all was forgiven. Suddenly, Gottehrer was being heralded as a genius and the best producer ever by both the band and Copeland.

When it came time to shoot the cover for *Beauty and the Beat*, photographer George DuBose got the job, accidentally. DuBose wanted to shoot the band for Andy Warhol's *Interview Magazine* but was told the Go-Go's didn't have time because they needed a cover for their new album. He ended up photographing the cover. The band wanted a timeless feel to the *Beauty and the Beat* cover. They also wanted a cover concept that would save them the trouble of having to decide what to wear; the cover featuring the girls in white bath towels and face masks achieved both these goals. They tried several things on their faces but ended up with Noxzema because it was the only thing that didn't crack immediately. The back of the album featured individual shots of the band members in the tub, shot in the bathroom of Wiedlin and Caffey's room at the Wellington, the hotel they were staying at while recording *Beauty and the Beat*. The cover received criticism from journalists like *New York Rocker*'s Don Snowden who wrongly assumed record execs, and not the

Go-Go's, had developed the concept. "It's a long way from the motley crew pictured on the Stiff single but if the Go-Go's want to come across as new wave cutie-pie heart-throbs, that's their business . . . But c'mon, the images—pouring bubbly in bubblebath, chocolates and trashy novels, hand on the telephone, the phallic rose—strike me as some 40-year old marketing exec's fantasy,"[4] Snowden wrote of the images on the album's back cover.

The album cover was the first time I saw what the Go-Go's looked like. I could finally put faces to my new heroes. In the days before social media, videos, and the internet, it was a lot harder to learn about your new favorite band. MTV would soon change that, but it wouldn't launch until a month after *Beauty and the Beat* was released. Years after I first discovered the Go-Go's, I was packing some records to move and noticed the similarities between the *Beauty and the Beat* cover and the cover of *Cut*, the debut album from the Slits. The Slits were naked except for loincloths and covered in mud, not Noxzema, but there was still the idea that both bands wanted to rebel against stereotypical, hypersexualized notions of what women should look like on an album cover. They were both powerful images that the bands chose themselves, which subverted the idea of how women should market their music. There was also the idea that the women wanted to conceal themselves, whether with face masks or mud, to keep a part hidden, especially from a music industry that wanted women to reveal themselves, and all of themselves, if they wanted to sell records.

* * *

As soon as the album was done, the Go-Go's hit the road. The tours and the venues kept getting bigger. The band went from being the house band at the Whisky and playing small clubs to opening for the Police for their *Ghost in the Machine* tour in less than a year. Miles Copeland also happened to be the manager of the Police. His brother, Stewart Copeland, was the drummer for the band. Not only would the Go-Go's end up on tour with the Police, but some extra money left over from the budget for a music video by the Police—$6,000 to be exact—paid for the Go-Go's first video, "Our Lips Are Sealed." The Go-Go's didn't understand the importance of video at the time; but when MTV launched in August 1981, they saw the difference it made. The girls goofed around in the video, driving around Los Angeles in a convertible, and splashing in a fountain. They hoped to get arrested for playing in the fountain, which they thought would make an exciting end to the video. The police didn't care, but the video would be played nonstop on MTV.

While the band was opening for the Police and playing sold-out stadiums, *Beauty and the Beat* went to number one on the *Billboard* album charts and would stay there for six weeks. *Beauty and the Beat* had passed *Ghost in the Machine* by tourmates the Police, which was at number six. Sting brought the girls a bottle of champagne to celebrate. Finally, the police were paying attention to the band, just not the ones they had hoped when they frolicked in that fountain in the "Our Lips Are Sealed" video. "We Got the Beat" went to number two and "Our Lips Are Sealed" to number twenty. The Go-Go's were everywhere, and *Beauty and the Beat* would go on to sell more than two million copies, making it one of the few debut albums to top the charts and putting the band on the same level as the Beatles and Elvis. *Beauty and the Beat* made the Go-Go's the first, and to date only, female band to have a number one album, who not only wrote their own songs but also played their own instruments. The album was not only a success, but "also a harbinger of what rock would become, and a bridge between punk, the movement whose rebelliousness had quashed the excesses of classic rock, and the genre-fusing music of the 1980s,"[5] said Hilary Hughes in her introduction to NPR's oral history of *Beauty and the Beat*.

On November 14, 1981, the Go-Go's appeared on *Saturday Night Live* with host Bernadette Peters and Billy Joel. Having to wait around the studio all day to play, the Go-Go's passed the time with alcohol and cocaine. By the time they took the stage, they were so drunk they could barely play. A clip of the performance is available online and worth the watch. The girls could not only hold their liquor on live TV, but the performance helped them sell a lot of records. All this attention helped to move the band's fan base beyond just college radio listeners and new-wave clubgoers. The band's fan base was now younger, especially attracting teen and pre-teen girls, who worshipped the band and didn't know what punk was, let alone about the band's punk roots. When the Go-Go's started they dreamed of spitting on Valley Girls, but those girls would soon be part of the band's fan base and the band would be part of a film that featured those girls they wanted to spit at. "We Got the Beat" would end up being the opening theme to the 1982 film *Fast Times at Ridgemont High*, a film that would popularize Valley Girls, mall culture, and Southern California teenage adolescence in the 1980s. The film launched Amy Heckerling's career, as well as the teen comedies of the 1980s from *Sixteen Candles* to *The Breakfast Club*.

A 1981 *Village Voice* poll put *Beauty and the Beat* in the number ten spot. Revisiting the album for an October 2019 review, *Pitchfork* gave it an 8.3. "Though it was a far cry from The Canterbury, *Beauty and the Beat* is about what's underneath the surface of pop music. Rather than relishing the California sunshine, the Go-Go's evoke *their* Los Angeles, a glittery, gritty place where punks rule the streets after dark."[6] Reviewing *Beauty and the Beat* in November 1981 for *Musician* magazine, Toby Goldstein said, "*Beauty and the Beat* is the album those of you who were embarrassed by pop music can use to say that pop's okay."[7] Wiedlin agreed with Goldstein's assessment. "One of my great quotes that I ever said, if I can quote myself, was I once compared The Go-Go's to Twinkies. I said, 'Everybody loves Twinkies, but they're ashamed to admit it,'"[8] she told *Songfacts* in 2007.

"I remember thinking if we sell 100,000 copies, that would be amazing. We had no idea it would do what it did. I look back even now and say *wow*. We went from zero to one hundred in about two years. And what happened with the album—its success—was beyond any of our expectations,"[9] said Carlisle. And while I don't like reducing the Go-Go's to sugary, sweet baked goods, that's a lot of Twinkies.

4
America's Sweethearts from Hell

When it came to marketing the band and *Beauty and the Beat*, the Go-Go's were promoted as fresh-faced, wholesome girls next door. "They're cute, they're bubbly, they throw nice little tantrums and then clean up after themselves"[1] is how a 1982 *Rolling Stone* cover story introduced the band. A 1980 *Record Mirror* piece started with the band bursting "on stage as bubbly as cheap champagne"[2] and later described them as "very Hollywood and very cute."[3] A review in *Newsday* talked about how "almost everything about the Go-Go's . . . is cute. The name is cute, the back-cover photos of the five female members of the band taking bubble baths are adorable."[4]

A 1981 *Creem* piece about the Go-Go's not only mentioned the *c* word (no, not that one; cute), but also included condescending titles ("Makeup Secrets of Five Wild & Crazy Girls") and sentences; "the group surprised an interesting mixture of teen magazine reporters and rock press by displaying an acute business sense, which several of the male writers didn't expect from five cute girls."[5] It then criticized the reporters and press in the room for not asking the band about their album and music but ended with a sexist line about "maybe there'll be a real sexy photo of the group accompanying this story, and that would definitely result in at least a few copies with sticky pages."[6] *Creem* criticized other media for not taking the band seriously, without acknowledging they were part of the problem too. At least, it was kinder than *Creem*'s 1977 review of *Queens of Noise* by the Runaways, which began with, "These bitches suck."[7]

"The Go-Go's *were* bright and bubbly but that's not all we were. We could've just as easily chosen the 'sexy' box but it wasn't in any of our natures. We were just a gang of young girls out having fun and at that time the media had to choose their box for us, so they chose 'girls next door,'"[8] said Wiedlin in a *Vogue* oral history of *Beauty and the Beat*. The fact that there were only two options or boxes for the Go-Go's to choose from shows the limited vocabulary that exists when talking about female musicians. There is the sexy girl or, at the very other end of the scale, the innocent girl next door. For the Go-Go's to be accepted by the media, music industry, and fans, they knew they had to choose one. They could be the good girls or the bad girls and, publicly at least, the Go-Go's were the good girls. "Guy bands were never described as perky and chirpy or adorable and cute. Increasingly, I read about us being frothy girl-pop and the band described as cheerleader-fun,"[9] Valentine wrote in her 2020 memoir of the disconnect between how the band saw themselves and how the media depicted the Go-Go's.

When they weren't being dismissed as cute, bubbly pop puppets, they were treated as a novelty act with no actual talent or smarts. "It sounds like a joyous, bubbling celebration by five cute girls, with no thought inside their darling little heads save for tonight's beach party,"[10] read the *NME* review of *Beauty and the Beat*. The Go-Go's played their own instruments and wrote their own music, but rather than focusing on how groundbreaking this was or treating the band with the respect they deserved, interviewers and reviewers usually focused on the girl's looks, clothes, or their love lives. "While there is ample sisterly affection, the Go-Go's keep plenty in reserve for their boyfriends,"[11] read a sexist, and extremely heteronormative, 1981 *People* interview. Over the years, members of the band have identified as bisexual, but that was left out of the band's narrative and the pages of *People*. "It bothers me when people say we're cute, bubbly girls. My God, it makes us sound like a bunch of air heads. Fun is not the only thing we think or write about,"[12] Carlisle told *Rolling Stone* in 1982. The same *Rolling Stone* piece described their tour bus as a "rolling sweet-sixteen bash."[13] The Go-Go's were marketed to their female teen and pre-teen fan base as the group of girls you would want to hang out with or have a sleepover party with even though the age range of band members in 1982 was twenty-two to twenty-eight. The media and music industry's desire to constantly infantilize female musicians is certainly not unique to the Go-Go's, but watching their gender constantly being referenced and all-girl being treated like a musical genre is so not cute. The Go-Go's were repeatedly asked what it was like to be in an all-girl band or what it was like to be a girl playing music. When they weren't being asked what it was like to be a girl in an all-girl band, they were asked patronizing questions like what their parents thought of what they were doing. Press on the Go-Go's often described the physical characteristics of band members before describing their sound. In some cases, there was more space devoted to talking about what band members were wearing than there was to their actual music. Interviews and profiles often commented on a band member's weight, especially when it came to lead singer Carlisle. She was described as "very pretty, but chubby"[14] in a 1981 *Boston Rock* piece. A 1982 *Washington Post* piece described her "baby-fattish face."[15]

There was also the assumption on the part of the media that the Go-Go's were manufactured or that they had slept their way to the top. Rick Springfield's album *Working Class Dog* was released the same year as *Beauty and the Beat*, but he was never asked if he slept his way to a record deal. To be fair, he did seem too busy with whatever was going on with Jessie's girl to socialize with record execs. Critics were often surprised to learn the Go-Go's didn't have a Svengali like Kim Fowley. The Runaways and Fowley were often mentioned in pieces about the Go-Go's showing both the one-in and one-out policy that applies to female musicians and the desire on the part of music critics to constantly compare female musicians to each other. In her 1981 *Boston Rock* piece, writer Julie Panebianco described a photographer who says of the Go-Go's, "They are like the Monkees. You wonder how long they looked for girls that all dressed like that,"[16] which echoed a lot of the writing about the Go-Go's at the time. The idea of the band as legitimate artists or serious songwriters was constantly dismissed. If they were good, there must have been a man behind them.

When *Beauty and the Beat* was released, the Go-Go's also had to bury a punk past that didn't fit with their bubbly pop present and their new broader more mainstream audience. The Go-Go's punk roots were often left out, downplayed, or treated like nothing more than a phase by the media and music industry. America's sweethearts certainly couldn't have a dark, angry punk past. The Los Angeles punk scene also wanted to distance itself from the Go-Go's punk roots. "*We Got the Neutron Bomb*, an oral history published in 2001 of the L.A. late '70's punk scene, briefly mentions The Go-Go's, but not without caveats about the band's careerism, poserdom, incompetence, and worst of all—gasp!—ambition,"[17] said Tracy Moore in her *Vanity Fair* piece on Ellwood's documentary.

Their punk past was not the only thing hidden. "The idea of being what we really were which was guzzling, foul mouthed, anything for a good time girls. I don't think people wanted that from us,"[18] Valentine told *Behind the Music*. Press and interviews for *Beauty and the Beat* promoted the Go-Go's as five squeaky-clean sisters who all got along and supported each other. The story of the Go-Go's is one of contradictions and for much of the band's career, the reality was much different than their sugar-coated image portrayed. Their hard partying was hidden, as was the infighting and the ego trips. Girls are supposed to be well-behaved, polite, seen and not heard. "America's Sweethearts from hell"[19] is how the band referred to themselves, Caffey told CBC's "Q" in a 2020 interview, which seemed like a much more accurate description of what was going on behind the scenes. During her time in the band, Caffey was a heroin addict who hid her addiction from her bandmates, the press, and the public. She often wore sunglasses and would alternate between heroin and cocaine to manage her addiction and the size of her pupils in public. Caffey went to rehab, two weeks after being kicked out of Ozzy Osbourne's dressing room on the Rock in Rio festival in January 1985. She now thanks the incident for helping her to get clean. Caffey was not the only Go-Go whose lips were sealed about her addiction. Carlisle had a $300 a day cocaine habit. While the press marketed the Go-Go's as one big singing sorority and potential pajama party friends for their teen fans, Carlisle kept a shoebox full of blow in her closet. (That sleepover would last for days and include little sleep!) The girls partied nonstop, drank to excess, and talked about getting off stage quickly so they could get off sexually. "In reality, they were a hard-drinking, pill-popping gang whose favourite on-tour pastime involved photographing each other's private parts and slipping the Polaroids under their road crew's hotel room doors. The crew had to guess which picture matched which Go-Go,"[20] recounted a 2002 Q magazine piece.

There are gendered standards when it comes to acceptable behavior from musicians and the culture of excess is something reserved for boys where it is not only accepted, but also celebrated. When it comes to male musicians, drug use is glamourized, romanticized, and viewed as a necessary part of the creative process. The debauchery and off-stage antics of male bands and musicians from Mötley Crüe to Ozzy Osbourne to Anthony Kiedis of the Red Hot Chili Peppers are well documented. Jokes are made about Keith Richards of the Rolling Stones still being alive or snorting his dad's ashes like cocaine. Aerosmith's Joe Perry and Steven Tyler wore their Toxic Twins nickname like a badge of honor.

The Go-Go's had to hide their partying and excess not only because it wasn't very ladylike, but because it wasn't part of the packaging of the band.

I recently rewatched *Amy*, the 2015 documentary about the late singer Amy Winehouse, and was troubled by footage that turned the singer's addictions and bulimia into jokes. Announcing the nominees for the fiftieth annual Grammy Awards in 2007, comedian George Lopez read Winehouse's name on the list of best female pop vocalist nominees and then made the joke, "Can someone wake her up this afternoon around six and tell her?"[21] He then called her a "drunk ass,"[22] while Foo Fighters members Dave Grohl and Taylor Hawkins laughed in the background. Winehouse had six nominations that year and beat Foo Fighters for Record of the Year for "Rehab." Later in the film, late-night comedian Jay Leno made a joke about how Winehouse's next album will feature "songs about cooking."[23] The punch line: "cooking crystal meth, black tar heroin."[24] Winehouse is just one example, but the media, the music industry, and late-night comedians love to mock, shame, and ridicule female musicians for their partying and their addictions.

"An addict male rock star may have maintained their credibility and authenticity, but addict female stars have been seen as lost cases, almost beyond help. This cultural image of an addict female artist has a well-established history from Billie Holiday to Amy Winehouse."[25] Male musicians who write about their addictions are labeled "honest" and "raw," while female musicians are "shocking" and "self-destructive." Women are expected to constantly apologize for their addiction, reveal their deepest secrets, and talk about the trauma behind their addictions. Men just have to cover the sex, drugs, and rock and roll. In the days before social media, *Us Weekly,* and gossip blogs, it was easier to keep a celebrity's private life hidden and out of the spotlight. "Thank god it was before mobile phones and social media and paparazzi, because we would've been the Lindsay Lohans of our time. We escaped that,"[26] Carlisle told NPR. Over the years, VH1's *Behind the Music*, which the girls aren't too fond of, memoirs from Valentine and Carlisle, interviews, and Ellwood's documentary would help to tell the story of what was really going on with the band.

*   *   *

Famed photographer Annie Leibovitz shot the group's first cover for *Rolling Stone* in 1982. The band was excited to be shooting with Leibovitz and although they initially objected to her idea to shoot them in white, Hanes, men's underwear, the girls eventually all agreed. The plain underwear didn't portray a hypersexual image, so they felt okay with the clothing choice. Unfortunately, the magazine decided to use the sexist "Go-Go's Put Out" coverline to accompany the image. As mentioned before, *Rolling Stone* may have promoted the Go-Go's as wholesome girls next door, but the magazine also welcomed any opportunity to exploit the band's sexuality to sell magazines. When the band complained about the cover, *Rolling Stone* publisher Jann Wenner told them they should be lucky to be on the cover at all. For their second *Rolling Stone* cover in 1984, the band was not photographed in underwear; instead, they're in slouchy sweaters and colourful socks, but they still received a sexist coverline treatment with "Women on Top." Let's look at some other *Rolling Stone* covers from that same year to see if there's a trend in their cover treatments.

March 1, 1984
Cover: The Police
Coverline: "An interview with Our Band of the Year"

June 7, 1984
Cover: Culture Club
Coverline: "Culture Club's Boy George. The *Rolling Stone* Interview"

June 21, 1984
Cover: Bob Dylan
Coverline: "Bob Dylan: The *Rolling Stone* Interview"

October 11, 1984
Cover: Tina Turner
Coverline: "She's Got Legs!"

November 22, 1984
Cover: Madonna
Coverline: "Madonna Goes All the Way"

What's a girl gotta do to get "The *Rolling Stone* Interview" treatment? This serious treatment is strictly for the boys. Keep in mind that women should feel lucky to be on the cover of *Rolling Stone* at all. While the Go-Go's had to put out for *Rolling Stone*, at least they got to wear that boring Hanes underwear. During the pop princess peak, hypersexualized images of young female musicians on the magazine's covers were the norm. According to a 2011 study, hypersexualized images of women represented six percent of *Rolling Stone* covers featuring women in the 1970s, but that number jumped to sixty-one percent in the 2000s.[27] In the late 1990s and early aughts, young women appeared on the cover in little clothing, in their underwear, or naked, often with a sheet, or some hands or, in the case of a 2002 Christina Aguilera cover, a guitar slightly obscuring their breasts. Women were sometimes posed with random phallic substitutes such as a hot dog, the neck of a guitar, or a dripping ice cream cone. *Rolling Stone* would never put a dick on the cover unless you count Donald Trump. Also, for *Rolling Stone*, the jailbait angle was okay. A coverline for a Lindsay Lohan cover read, "Hot, Ready and Legal!" I know they're not musicians, but the Olsen Twins cover featured, "America's Favourite Fantasy." Lohan had just turned eighteen and Ashley and Mary-Kate were seventeen at the time the issues were published.

I'm all for women appearing on the cover of a magazine on their own terms, but pop princesses were conditioned to believe these hypersexualized images were necessary to sell their music, their films, or their fragrance lines. They knew the covers provided a perfect opportunity for them to shed their skin, to reveal a shiny new image, or to show they were no longer beholden to the cult of Disney. Britney Spears appeared on the cover of *Rolling Stone* in 1999 in bed and in her underwear with a bare midriff and a Teletubby. Some stories about the photo shoot have said Spears was uncomfortable, some have said it was her idea, and some have said it was suggested to Spears at the shoot that she portray a more provocative image for the photos that would set her apart from Debbie Gibson who she was being compared to at the time. *Framing Britney Spears*, the 2021 *New York Times* documentary, suggested Spears was always in control of her sexuality from day one, an argument I am not sure I entirely agree with but felt like if I didn't, I was just as misogynistic as the creepy male journalists in the film who asked her about her boob job or the people who shame her on Instagram for posting topless photos. "They were really cool but I didn't really know what the hell I was doing. And, to be totally honest with you, at the time I was 16, so I really didn't. I was back in my bedroom, and I had my little sweater on and he was like, 'Undo your sweater a little bit more,'"[28] Spears said in a 2003 interview of the cover shoot. Reading that quote it's hard not to be skeptical of the way that *Framing Britney Spears* positioned Spears' sexuality. Writer and former *Rookie* editor Tavi Gevinson summed it up best in a piece on Spears for *The Cut*. "[I]t is absurd to discuss her image from that time as though there was not an apparatus behind it, as though she existed in a vacuum where she was figuring out her sexuality on her own terms, rather than in an economy where young women's sexuality is rapidly commodified until they are old enough to be discarded."[29]

The Spears cover also didn't exist in a vacuum. *Rolling Stone* had a pattern when it came to coverage of pop princesses. Debating whose idea the shoot was, pulls the focus from a corporate magazine that sexualized and sacrificed young women for capitalism. *Rolling Stone* was certainly not the only one to do that, but the magazine's continued sexualization of young women is worth noting. The fact that Spears was repeatedly asked by the media about her virginity and told reporters she was saving herself for someone special might have also made photo shoots like the *Rolling Stone* cover seem justifiable. She may have been posing in her bedroom in short shorts and a bra, but she was still a virgin and wasn't doing the actual deed so what's the damage?

Sexist cover treatments and coverlines were certainly not limited to *Rolling Stone*, a cover of *Record* magazine featured a picture of the Go-Go's accompanied by the coverline "Go-Go's Ready for Some Action." The male musicians included on the cover were treated with much more respect, "After a Fashion: Stepping Way Out with Joe Jackson," sold one story, and "Marvin Gaye an Artist's Legacy," promoted another. But as one of the largest and most popular music and pop culture magazines, *Rolling Stone* certainly set the tone and direction for how female musicians were covered. In a 2018 *Vanity Fair* oral history on the women who changed *Rolling Stone* in the 1970s, editor Christine Doudna talked about "trying to get some rock critic to try to change the word 'girl group'— because we all wanted to be *women* at this point."[30] The fact that the *Rolling Stone* office also had a sign that said "Boys' Club" probably did little to help with office culture and respect for both female employees and the female musicians they covered.

Thankfully, this club was about to be challenged by a new promotional tool for musicians, one that would benefit female bands like the Go-Go's.

5
Step Aside REO Speedwagon

A year before the Go-Go's had the beat, Pat Benatar released her second album *Crimes of Passion* on August 5, 1980. The album entered the *Billboard* charts the week of August 23 and reached the number two spot in January 1981. It held this spot for five weeks just behind John Lennon and Yoko Ono's *Double Fantasy*. *Crimes of Passion* sold more than four million copies in the United States and earned Benatar her first Grammy win in 1981. The album included "Hit Me with Your Best Shot," which reached number nine on the *Billboard* charts and is one of the singer's most popular songs. Benatar no longer performs the song live, and she dropped it from her set list in 2022 out of respect to the victims of mass shootings. "[The title] is tongue-in-cheek, but you have to draw the line. I can't say those words out loud with a smile on my face, I just can't,"[1] she said in July 2022. Like the Go-Go's, it took Benatar far too long to be included in the Rock & Roll Hall of Fame. She was nominated in 2000, after being eligible for over a decade, and finally inducted in 2022 with a class that included Dolly Parton, Carly Simon, and Annie Lennox (for the Eurythmics).

I will also always have a soft spot for Benatar because even though I often forget my computer password, I can still remember, and perform, the choreography from her "Love Is a Battlefield" video forty years later.

In her 2010 autobiography *Between a Heart and a Rock Place*, Benatar talked about the marketing for *Crimes of Passion*. Chrysalis, her record label, took out a full-page ad in *Billboard* to promote the album. "They had taken the cover photo to the album and airbrushed off the tank top I was wearing. In its place, they'd put a sign over my seemingly nude chest that announced the release date of the new record. As if that weren't enough, they'd also given me a boob job,"[2] she said. Benatar had already clashed with Chrysalis over the album's cover art. The label wanted the cover to feature only Benatar, while she wanted a shot that included both her and her band. A compromise was reached that would feature Benatar solo on the front, while the band would appear on the back of the album. This was not the only album cover Benatar clashed with record execs over. She also talked in her book about the lengthy discussions and compromises that surrounded the cover of 1982's *Get Nervous*. In her 2019 memoir *Face It*, Blondie's Debbie Harry talked about sexist marketing campaigns and similar fights with record labels and execs over the fact that Blondie was a band and not just a female singer. She recounted a record company promotion for Blondie's first album that used an image of her in a see-through blouse, despite earlier reassurances that only headshots would be used and that all band members would be included. "Sex sells, that's what they say, and I'm not stupid, I know that. But on my terms, not some executive's,"[3] she said in *Face It*. When Blondie's record label placed an ad to promote her 1976 single "Rip Her to Shreds," it featured a picture of Blondie with the text, "Wouldn't You Like to Rip Her to Shreds?" Blondie was furious when she saw the ad.

There is no shortage of stories in Benatar's memoir about the sexism she experienced in the music industry in the early 1980s, from DJs that wanted her to sit on their laps to get her records played to press releases that focused heavily on her sexuality. "And women? They weren't equals, they weren't rock stars, they weren't players. Women were girlfriends or groupies,"[4] Benatar said of the industry's misogyny. The fact that women like Benatar and the Go-Go's achieved success in such a challenging and misogynistic industry puts them in my hall of fame forever. "We'd be pushing to get airtime for our songs, and radio programmers would say things like, 'We'll definitely put that single in heavy rotation at the end of the week, but we can't right now. We're already playing a single by a girl,'"[5] Benatar recounted in *Between a Heart and a Rock Place*. Michael Plen, I.R.S. head of promotions, experienced similar problems when he tried to get radio play for the Go-Go's. "I remember going early on to local radio stations, and the DJs would just be, like, 'Girls? What a joke,'"[6] Wiedlin told *Goldmine* magazine. "And even when we started to be on the radio, they would have just one slot for the girl rocker or the girl singer,"[7] said Caffey. That one-slot policy also applied to concert and festival lineups. And while Benatar didn't have to hide her partying like the Go-Go's did, she did have to downplay the fact that she had children, because being a mom wasn't considered sexy to the record-buying public. She was also encouraged to get back to work and return to touring as soon as possible after having her kids so fans wouldn't forget about her.

Precious Time, Benatar's third album, was released in July 1981, the same month as *Beauty and the Beat*. The year also featured albums by other female artists like Sheena Easton, Chaka Khan, Kim Carnes, Olivia Newton-John, and Stevie Nicks. Despite this, male musicians and bands still ruled the album charts and the press in 1981 from *Hi Infidelity* by REO Speedwagon to *Paradise Theatre* by Styx to *Tattoo You* by the Rolling Stones, and *4* by Foreigner. Of the *Billboard* number one albums of the year (twelve in total), only three were by female artists (Carnes, Benatar, and Nicks), four if you count *Double Fantasy* by Lennon and Ono, which you should because Ono has been vilified so much over the years by fans, the press, and the music industry that she should get all the credit and props she so rightly deserves.

Beauty and the Beat reached number one on the *Billboard* charts on March 6, 1982, where it stayed for six weeks. It was eventually knocked out of the top spot by the *Chariots of Fire* soundtrack. The Go-Go's were the only female musicians who topped the album charts that year. If not for the Go-Go's, the 1982 album charts would have been entirely dominated by male musicians from John Cougar and Men at Work to Asia and The J. Geils Band. When Cougar appeared on the cover of *Rolling Stone* he, of course, received "The *Rolling Stone* Interview" cover treatment. He did not have to "put out" like the Go-Go's did. Fleetwood Mac's *Mirage* did reach the number one spot for five weeks in 1982, but that band was not all-female, even though Lindsey Buckingham or Mick Fleetwood being kicked of the band was an attractive option for Stevie Nicks and Christine McVie at various points in the band's, to put it mildly, complicated history.

Laura Brannigan, Joan Jett, and Donna Summer may have joined the Go-Go's on the list of the top 100 songs of 1982, but the singles charts were still largely dominated by men. "We Got the Beat," the Go-Go's biggest hit, went to number two on the *Billboard* Hot 100 charts, just behind "I Love Rock 'n Roll" by Joan Jett & the Blackhearts, and spent three weeks there. On *Billboard*'s year-end chart of the top pop singles, it was number twenty-five. "Our Lips Are Sealed" was number twenty on the *Billboard* Hot 100 charts and number fifteen on the *Billboard* Top Rock Tracks. In total, "Our Lips Are Sealed" spent thirty weeks on the *Billboard* charts, which was impressive for a debut single. *Rolling Stone* named "Our Lips Are Sealed" one of the 100 Greatest Pop Songs of all time. The success of the Go-Go's and *Beauty and the Beat* paved the way for other female artists like Cyndi Lauper, Madonna, and Tina Turner who topped the charts later in the 1980s. "In 1983, Cyndi Lauper had a massive hit with 'Girls Just Want to Have Fun,' but the Go-Go's and their legion of predominantly female teenage fans were already peeing in the bushes at that party, on a quest for another bottle of Bacardi,"[8] read a 2016 *Newsweek* piece that called the Go-Go's "the ideal soundtrack to suburban teen rebellion."[9] For me, they definitely were. Reviewing the Go-Go's third album *Talk Show* in 1984, the *Washington Post* said, "Cyndi Lauper may have had the hit with 'Girls Just Want to Have Fun,' but it was the Go-Go's who best articulated the sentiment as a rock and roll esthetic."[10]

*   *   *

"Ladies and gentlemen, rock 'n' roll," those were the first words heard when MTV went on the air at 12:01 a.m. on August 1, 1981. They were followed by the first video played, the tongue in cheek "Video Killed the Radio Star" by the Buggles. At the time, the station was only available in smaller markets like Tulsa and Wichita and not in major centers like New York City or Los Angeles. By the time I got MTV in Canada, where I live, it had replaced music videos with catfishes, teen moms, and GTL (gym, tan, laundry). We had a Canadian equivalent in MuchMusic which launched in 1984 and played videos and local video shows like *Video Hits* and *4 O'Clock Rock*, as well as US shows like *Friday Night Videos*. My friends and I were obsessed with *Friday Night Videos* and traded VHS tapes back and forth of the videos we recorded from the show. Weekend sleepovers were spent watching Duran Duran's "Hungry Like the Wolf" video and debating which member of Duran Duran was the cutest (Simon, of course).

The second video that aired after "Video Killed the Radio Star" was "You Better Run" by Benatar, which makes her the first female musician played on MTV. The station's first day also included an eclectic mix of Split Enz, Fleetwood Mac, Blondie, eleven Rod Stewart videos, and lots of REO Speedwagon. "You Better Run" was Benatar's cover of a 1966 song by the Young Rascals and was included on *Crimes of Passion*. Chrysalis approached Benatar and the band about shooting a live performance video for MTV. Many of the videos in the network's early days were live performance videos because they were all that was available, and the future of music videos was still largely unknown. MTV didn't have enough videos to fill the 24-hour format when it launched, so "You Better Run" was on heavy rotation in the station's early days. "But the executives behind MTV were in such a mad scramble to get their new cable channel up and running that it never occurred to them to question whether there were sufficient videos by Journey, Loverboy, and Rod Stewart to fill out 24 hours of airtime,"[11] wrote Lori Majewski and Jonathan Bernstein in the introduction to *Mad World: An Oral History of New Wave Artists and Songs That Defined the 1980s*. European bands like Duran Duran, Culture Club, and the Eurythmics would eventually help MTV fill the airtime.

"The Go-Go's and MTV came up at the perfect time for each other,"[12] said former MTV VJ Martha Quinn in Ellwood's documentary *The Go-Go's*. *Beauty and the Beat* was released just one month before MTV launched. The video for "Our Lips Are Sealed" was a hit and played nonstop on MTV. "That's how a lot of young people found out about us. Relentless touring and being dumped into people's living rooms on MTV,"[13] Valentine told the *Los Angeles Times*. "The Go-Go's would never have had the success we did without MTV."[14] The band also released a popular video for "We Got the Beat," which featured a live performance filmed in December 1981 at Palos Verdes High School in Los Angeles. Video's reliance on image put even more pressure on musicians. Bands like Journey and REO Speedwagon who had been popular on the radio now found that their look did not translate well to video. When people wanted their MTV, they didn't want them on it. While bands that traditionally had been excluded from radio benefited from MTV and proved popular with viewers. "Prior to MTV, the game was all about radio,"[15] said Miles Copeland in *We Got the Neutron Bomb: The Untold Story of L.A. Punk* and because punk music wasn't radio friendly, and many established bands initially refused to make videos, MTV promoted the musicians and artists who did. "And in return, the punk bands paid attention to MTV, because they were one of the few people who would play their stuff. And the Go-Go's totally benefitted from this."[16]

MTV also benefited from the Go-Go's whose videos were not only popular with viewers, but also opened the door for other female musicians. Artists like Madonna and Lauper may have been big on MTV, but they would not have achieved that success if the Go-Go's hadn't been in constant rotation in the station's early days. The Go-Go's initially objected to filming the video for "Our Lips Are Sealed" because they thought it was a waste of time, but the investment paid off. The video contributed to the band's image as the fun girls you wanted to hang out with. My friends and I even tried to replicate the video's ending where the five Go-Go's frolicked in the Electric Fountain on the corner of Wilshire and Santa Monica in downtown Los Angeles, but our fountain was much closer to home. It was at a suburban mall where we pooled our babysitting money to buy frothy Orange Julius drinks and chocolate chip muffins from Marvellous Mmmuffins, a Canadian mall food court staple in the 1980s. "It was half-baked and low budget, and I remember thinking, why are we aimlessly driving around in this cool car . . . I hated it until we got to the scene where we were playing live at the Viper Room, because it was really important that people saw us with instruments. That was the only part that made sense to me,"[17] Valentine told the *Los Angeles Times*. There was still the perception that the Go-Go's, and other female musicians, didn't play the instruments on their albums, so it was important to show them playing a guitar or the drums whenever possible. "It put the Go-Go's on the map,"[18] Carlisle told *Vulture* in 2021. "It felt like California. And it beautifully sums up the essence of the band. We're irreverent and self-deprecating, and you can see that in the video. We just didn't give a shit, really. I think that's one of the things about the Go-Go's that people do respond to."[19]

Music charts weren't calculated electronically in the 1980s, so it took longer for artists to determine if a song or album was taking off. They had to rely on radio and live shows. The number of people in a crowd was a measure of how you were performing as a musician. MTV added a new source, and measure, of success. Artists who had videos played on MTV found their record sales increased, as stores received requests for artists that weren't being played on the radio but were being played on MTV. The Stray Cats and Devo are examples of bands that weren't getting radio play, but experienced increased sales because of video rotation on MTV. "By 1983, a Neilsen survey commissioned by MTV owner, Warner-Amex, showed MTV to be influencing 63% of its viewers to buy certain albums."[20] Record companies who initially didn't want to provide MTV with free videos from their artists soon started to see the benefits. MTV also changed the demographics of concertgoers. According to Benatar, there was a distinct shift in women attending her concerts once her videos started airing on MTV. "When we first began, most of our concerts were probably 80/20 male-oriented. There were very few women. Very few women used to go to concerts no matter who was playing, male or female. I saw that really change about 1982,"[21] said Benatar in 1987.

In the 1980s, women like the Go-Go's, Joan Jett, Pat Benatar, Cyndi Lauper, Madonna, and Tina Turner not only found success on MTV, but also created some of the most innovative and popular videos of the decade. "The ladies of 80s music videos brought forth new visual representations of women including: experiences in the workforce, issues of class, messages of power, and unique expressions of love and sex. In the infancy of MTV video, female artists created a complex pattern of images that underscored lyrics of power and individuality,"[22] said critic Gwen Hofmann in a 2016 *Bitch Flicks* piece on ladies of the 1980s. *She's So Unusual*, Lauper's debut album, stayed in the top thirty on the album charts for over sixty weeks and included four top-five singles. A large part of this success was attributed to Lauper's popular music videos, particularly the video for the album's first single "Girls Just Want to Have Fun," which was released in 1983 on MTV. Originally, the song featured different lyrics, but Lauper altered them to make the song more of a feminist anthem about the inequality women face. The singer also played a significant role in the look and feel of the music video. *Like a Virgin*, Madonna's 1984 album, sold more than three million copies in fourteen weeks and was triple platinum before the singer had even toured, based on the success of the singer's videos on MTV. "The 1985 winner of the top Grammy award, Tina Turner, had no record deal one year but a top hit single the next. Her album, *Private Dancer*, has sold ten million copies around the world. Pat Benatar, Chaka Khan, and the Pointer Sisters all reached a million in sales with albums promoted by music video," wrote Lisa Lewis in *Jump Cut*.[23] As some of the first women to have success on MTV, the Go-Go's increased visibility for female artists on the channel and showed the opportunities and possibilities for women and video. Madonna would not have been able to frolic on a gondola in her "Like a Virgin" video if the Go-Go's had not frolicked in a fountain for "Our Lips Are Sealed" first.

A March 1985 *Newsweek* cover featured Lauper accompanied by the coverline, "Rock and Roll Woman Power."[24] The cover story talked about how "Cyndi Lauper and Madonna are reinventing pop's feminine mystique with hot videos and wild styles."[25] While the story talked about how women topped the charts in 1985, the same tired misogyny still greeted female musicians. In her 2012 memoir, Lauper talked about the manufactured rivalry between her and Madonna that existed in the 1980s, two decades later the media and music industry would do the same thing to Christina Aguilera and Britney Spears.

When I became famous—I mean right away—the press always asked me about one person: Madonna. They tried to create this big rivalry . . . even her record company got in on it. They ran an ad in *Billboard* where she was dressed in a white corset. And it said something like,

"This girl's gonna give Cyndi Lauper a run for her money."[26]

In the *Newsweek* piece, Madonna talked about the sexism she experienced and the double standard that existed for female musicians when it came to sexuality. "When someone like Prince, Elvis, or Jagger does the same thing, they are being honest, sensual human beings. But when I do it: 'Oh please, Madonna, you're setting the women's movement back a million years.'"[27]

While MTV in the 1980s promoted female musicians, the station was often criticized for its lack of Black artists. After a 1983 interview, David Bowie called MTV out for its lack of racial diversity and for not playing Black artists, or if they did, they aired them in the early morning hours when few people were watching. "After the interview, he asks me, 'Why do you think MTV doesn't play black music?' I said, 'We try to play music for a particular type of demographic and genre.' He said, 'What about all the black kids?' I said, 'You got to talk to MTV about that.' I got hung out to dry,"[28] VJ Mark Goodman said of the now infamous interview with Bowie. MTV's excuse was that Black artists didn't play "rock" music, which was the station's focus and format. MTV's lack of racial diversity also extended to the actual video content. In *She's A Rebel*, writer Gillian G. Gaar talked about Donna Summer's video for "She Works Hard for the Money." "*Rock & Roll Confidential* reported in 1983 that Keith Williams, who had written the script for the Donna Summer video 'She Works Hard for the Money' had been told to focus on a white family in the video 'for MTV.'"[29]

It's also important to remember that while MTV featured videos by women musicians, it also played plenty of other videos that included sexist portrayals of women. The objectification of women in music videos has been widely documented and not just by Tipper Gore and the Parents Music Resource Centre, who were very active in the 1980s on issues like sexist music videos and offensive lyrics. From Tawny Kitaen doing the splits on the hood of a car in a Whitesnake video to the girls in ZZ Top's video for "Legs," women in videos were portrayed as nothing more than bangable flesh props. MTV started to move away from music videos in 1992 and embraced reality programming like *The Real World*, which premiered that year and is often regarded as the first reality show. "One of the signature things that happened that year was that Bill Clinton was a constant presence on MTV in 1990-91, and he was elected president,"[30] Mark Tannenbaum told NPR in 2011. "Once you've helped elect a U.S. president, are you gonna go back to playing Winger videos?"[31] added Craig Marks. Tannenbaum and Marks coauthored *I Want My MTV: The Uncensored Story of the Music Video Revolution*.

When MTV stopped playing videos, it signaled the 1980s were over. It was also the end for some artists who were popular at the start of the decade. A groundbreaking video featuring a pep rally turned riot and some anarchist cheerleaders didn't help. REO Speedwagon's Kevin Cronin of the end of videos on MTV said:

For us, there was a direct correlation between that and "Smells Like Teen Spirit." I thought that video was awesome, but it was a death knell for us temporarily. We went from headlining sold-out arenas to playing the Clark County Fair somewhere in Missouri with a freaking Ferris wheel in the distance. We owned the '80s. Well, you can't own forever.[32]

6
The F-Word

"5 Girls, No Men." That's how an American newspaper started its review of *Beauty and the Beat*. The review went on to suggest that the band and the album would be a success because the Go-Go's weren't "radical feminists." At the time, the Go-Go's didn't consider themselves feminists at all. "Through the years I've been asked 'were you feminists?' We were, I realize it now cause of our attitudes, but we weren't 'we're going to do this against the guys and, you know, fuck them,' we weren't like that at all. We thought anything was possible, including succeeding in an industry that was run by men,"[1] Carlisle said in Ellwood's documentary. The Los Angeles punk scene that birthed the Go-Go's was an encouraging community for female musicians. Women had already claimed their space in the scene when the Go-Go's arrived in 1978. Regularly seeing female musicians like Alice Bag and Exene Cervenka of the band X on stage made women playing music feel less like a revolutionary or political act and more like just another Tuesday night at the Masque. Outside their punk bubble, things weren't as welcoming. The Go-Go's fought for inclusion in an industry that treated women making music like nothing more than a passing fad. "We just plunged in with the attitude that we're going to do this and we're going to do it well,"[2] said Wiedlin in a 1980 interview with *Sounds*.

The idea of starting a band, picking up an instrument and learning to play, figuring out how to write your own songs, and not giving up when skinheads spit at you because you're not the Specials. What's more feminist than that? The Go-Go's believed they could be as good as male musicians and didn't let anything stop them. At the time the Go-Go's were shopping for a record deal, labels refused to sign all-girl bands because they didn't have a proven track record when it came to success. The Go-Go's changed that. The band proved that an all-girl group could not only sell records but could be successful. "For the first time, there were five females that played their own instruments, wrote their own songs, had control of their own identity, were managed by a female manager, and were able to achieve monumental success by being themselves. From a gender standpoint, it's amazing, and it leads to a change,"[3] said Richard Gottehrer, *Beauty and the Beat* producer, in the NPR oral history of the album.

The Go-Go's were a feminist band, even if they never explicitly adopted the label. The "attitude" Carlisle referred to in Ellwood's documentary was feminist, it just wasn't cool to call it that at the time. When *Beauty and the Beat* was released in 1981, the feminist label might have alienated fans and critics who thought it was a dirty word that implied an us-versus-them dynamic, much like Carlisle's description does in the earlier quote. The Go-Go's also existed at a time when to be accepted so-called cute bubblegum pop stars couldn't have a political message. That's not the case now; we see it in musicians like Lizzo and Lady Gaga, but when *Beauty and the Beat* was released pop and politics mixing, especially for women, was as unlikely as 1981-era MTV playing a musician who wasn't white. Folk singers were political; pop stars weren't. At the time, being a feminist band implied a group of angry man-haters which the Go-Go's were not. "I think we were afraid of being labeled feminists . . . But actions mean more than words and we controlled ourselves, took what we wanted, and didn't get successful based on hypersexuality as so many people have I feel been forced to do. That in itself makes us feminists,"[4] Wiedlin said in the *Vogue* oral history of *Beauty and the Beat*. The Go-Go's broke records and barriers for other women in music. They are still the only all-female band who wrote their own music and played their own instruments to have a *Billboard* number one album—no other band has achieved this. I keep repeating this fact throughout the book because it is a groundbreaking achievement, especially when you look at the challenges and misogyny the band faced and the landscape that existed for female musicians in 1978, which was bleaker than an REO Speedwagon power ballad. The Go-Go's should also be celebrated for being a punk band that went on to achieve mainstream pop success. And while bands in the 1970s Los Angeles punk scene might have argued they didn't want success, the Go-Go's forging their own path despite criticism and rejection from the scene that once supported them was both fearless and feminist.

The Bangles came close to the Go-Go's historic number one album achievement, making it to number two in

1986 with *Different Light* but endured constant comparisons to the Go-Go's by critics and a music industry who thought the Bangles could only achieve success because the Go-Go's had broken up. Remember, only one female band can exist at a time. "Are the Bangles the new Go-Go's? One can't help but wonder. After all, like the Go-Go's, the Bangles are an all-female rock band that plays Sixties-style, Beatles-influenced rock," opened Michael Goldberg's September 1984 *Rolling Stone* article on the Bangles. Music journalists regularly compared the two bands, which showed the limited frames of reference that existed for women making music, as well as helped to manufacture a rivalry between the Go-Go's and the Bangles.

"We want people to remember how we managed to make it in a man's world. It was hard. People were openly and blatantly sexist in those days. The industry is still run by the patriarchy, but people are way more cautious about being open about it—at least they know they might be wrong. And girl power was really important,"[5] said Wiedlin in a 2021 *USA Today* piece. The Go-Go's were girl power before girl power existed. They were unapologetic and brash, qualities associated with girl power and the riot grrrls of the 1990s. The Go-Go's also embraced the same DIY spirit and punk roots as riot grrrl bands like Bikini Kill and Heavens to Betsy. When the Go-Go's started, they were the original riot grrrls.

*   *   *

Riot grrrl started in the Pacific Northwest, specifically Olympia, Washington, in the early 1990s, a decade after

Beauty and the Beat was released. The underground movement combined music, feminism, and punk. Like the Go-Go's, riot grrrls believed they should be able to express themselves in the same way as men. Riot grrrls wrote songs about rape, abuse, activism, class, race, and sexuality, subject matter that was more overtly political than what the Go-Go's were singing about. The Go-Go's weren't all froth though, and *Beauty and the Beat* had political songs like "This Town" and "Can't Stop the World," the politics just weren't as in your face as they were with riot grrrl bands. Bikini Kill's Tobi Vail referenced the Go-Go's in her zine *Jigsaw*. "First of all, I would like to inform you that the Go-Go's don't suck so stop putting them down. YES that means you Mr./Ms. rock journalist,"[6] she said in *Jigsaw* #2. Her defense of the band went on to discuss how girls with guitars are "threatening to the power structures"[7] and how "we are told that there are never any good girl bands and are deprived of our heroines!"[8] The Go-Go's might not have been publishing zines like *Jigsaw* or engaging in direct political action in the way women like Vail and Bikini Kill's Kathleen Hanna were, but riot grrrls wouldn't have existed had the Go-Go's not paved the way first. Both the Go-Go's and the riot grrrls embraced the idea of just picking up a guitar and doing it, whether you were any good or not. Watching an early clip of the Go-Go's performing at the Masque in what was their first or second show, I could easily have envisioned Bikini Kill being the next band to play on the bill. Riot grrrl also represented an attempt to subvert the word "girl." The word was constantly used to describe the Go-Go's, whether they were "good girls," "wholesome girls," or "girls next door" their gender was constantly acknowledged. Riot grrrls wanted to challenge how "girl" was used and reclaim it as their own.

Many of the bands riot grrrls cited as influences, from the Slits to X-Ray Spex, were contemporaries, and influences, of the Go-Go's. There's a tendency when writing about women making music to treat it like a novelty and not acknowledge legacy, influence, or history. Like the Raincoats had never existed or PJ Harvey had never picked up a guitar. Each female musician is treated like something new, her ties to the past severed and her connections to the future denied. What Vail referred to in *Jigsaw* when she talked about being "deprived of our heroines."[9] When the media wrote about riot grrrl, the term served as both an easy identifier and a dismissive critique. Riot grrrl was often reduced to a musical genre, stripped of its politics and message. Female musicians were also called riot grrrls even if they didn't self-identify. Hole's Courtney Love was often called a riot grrrl even though she has been vocal about the fact that she is not. Riot grrrl became a catchall for any angry girl with a guitar or a microphone. Riot grrrls eventually declared a media boycott, after constantly being dismissed and ridiculed by the press. "In 1992, *Newsweek*, along with other mainstream magazines and newspapers, brought riot grrrl into the homes of suburban teenagers who needed it, but it also misrepresented many of the movement's goals and brought a level of attention that many of the girls didn't want,"[10] Lisa Darms said in her introduction to *The Riot Grrrl Collection*. When they were covered, the focus was often on the girls' appearances and what they wore, with little attempt made to engage with the actual music or its message. It's like the approach journalists took with the Go-Go's. Riot grrrls were misquoted, taken out of context, and treated with condescension. "Feminist Riot Grrrls Don't Just Wanna Have Fun,"[11] read a headline on a *USA Today* piece. The piece opened with, "Better watch out, boys. From hundreds of once pink, frilly bedrooms, comes the young feminist revolution. And it's not pretty. But it doesn't wanna be. So there!"[12] It goes on to describe riot grrrls as "punkettes"[13] and "self-absorbed."[14] The Slits were also called "punkettes" and hated it as much as the riot grrrls did.

A sidebar described the movement's fashion and look as "unshaven armpits and legs, heavy, black Doc Martens boots, fishnet stockings and garter belts under baggy army shorts."[15] In *Girls to the Front*, her history of riot grrrl, author Sara Marcus described how the writer of a *Spin* magazine piece on riot grrrl initially found her piece accompanied by "a photograph of a topless girl with her hands covering her breasts and the word BITCH written across her chest."[16] The writer also had to fight to stop a copy editor from correcting the spelling of "grrrl" to "girl" but found an ally in an editor who argued that *Spin* would never have corrected the spelling of the band Phish. Of course not, they're dudes. The media often didn't understand the reasons behind why riot grrrls wrote a word like "slut" on their bodies and treated the felt marker scrawls like nothing more than a fashion accessory, focusing on style over substance.

Riot grrrl contributed to the impression of the 1990s as a progressive time for women. The movement was often associated with the grunge scene, which also originated in the Pacific Northwest in the early 1990s and was regarded as a supportive scene for women, even if women never reached the level of success that male grunge bands like Nirvana or Pearl Jam did. Female bands from L7 to Babes in Toyland sold less records than their male counterparts and got less press and less money. Just because Kurt Cobain and Eddie Vedder championed Shonen Knife and Sonic Youth or wore Rock for Choice shirts didn't mean women in music weren't still being objectified or that misogyny didn't exist. Despite what Gen X nostalgia (of which I am guilty of), *Spin* Women in Music issues, and Lilith Fair might tell you, the alternative music scene in the early to mid-1990s was not about a girl.

* * *

Not only has the Go-Go's legacy as feminists been downplayed, by both the band and others, but the Go-Go's influence on female musicians is often overlooked. "Songs like 'We Got the Beat' were built with a timeless durability as solidly constructed as a Motown hit. But to this day, the Go-Go's music tends to be dismissed as frothy and cute, when in fact, the band was a paradigm shifter,"[17] Evelyn McDonnell wrote in the *New York Times*. The Go-Go's were trailblazers and no album by the band exemplified this spirit more than *Beauty and the Beat*. Girls picking up guitars didn't begin with Courtney Love or Sleater-Kinney or Veruca Salt; it started with the Go-Go's. Feminist anthems like Bikini Kill's "Rebel Girl" or the Spice Girls' "Wannabe" would not exist without the punk power anthem "We Got the Beat." Riot grrrls made feminism cool for young women and the Spice Girls made feminism cool for their younger sisters, but none of this would have happened without Belinda, Kathy, Jane, Gina, and Charlotte.

"We were five really strong, kind of bull-headed women, together, and I think the energy we created—it was so pro-women and so powerful. At the time, we discounted it, and it was important. We changed things for hundreds of thousands of girls. When I think about that, that's probably what I'm most proud of: we changed possibilities for girls,"[18] said Wiedlin in the NPR oral history of *Beauty and the Beat*. One of the musicians who counts the Go-Go's as an influence is Bikini Kill's Kathleen Hanna. "As a young girl going into a space where women owned the stage, and owned it unapologetically like they were born to be there—to me, it represented a moment of possibility,"[19] Hanna said of seeing a Go-Go's concert in 1982. Like Hanna, the Go-Go's opened a world of possibilities for me. Had it not been for the Go-Go's I never would have had the courage to pick up an instrument, start a band, or pick up a pen, in the days before computers, and start writing. *Beauty and the Beat* still inspires me today, the same way it did when I first heard it. Like Hanna, seeing the Go-Go's command the stage empowered me. I saw that women could be something more than just a vocalist or a backup singer, that they could play instruments, that they could form a musical girl gang, and that they could achieve success in a world that wanted to hold them down. "I've always loved that they were an all-girl rock band—of course—but also how interconnected they are with punk subculture. As I got to know a bit more about their history I can't help but feel it informed a lot of my goals and ideals,"[20] Danielle Haim, lead guitarist and singer of Haim, told *Vogue*.

The Linda Lindas have not only listed the Go-Go's as an inspiration, but also covered their song "Tonite," the third track from *Beauty and the Beat*, and have confessed to playing more songs by the Go-Go's than any other band. In a 2019 radio interview, Valentine told a story about Courtney Love being a fan of the Go-Go's. Love is rumored to have said that if it wasn't for the Go-Go's she wouldn't be here. Love's famous husband Kurt Cobain was also rumored to be a fan of the Go-Go's. A December 1994 issue of *Raygun* magazine compared the impact of *Beauty and the Beat* to that of Nirvana's *Nevermind*. "Like Nirvana, the Go-Go's succeeded in turning the music world upside down, permanently changing the face of mainstream pop."[21] The bands were also united by the fact that they both faced criticism from the community they had originated in, accused of selling out, and capitalizing on mainstream success. Love's Hole bandmate, bassist Melissa Auf der Maur, was also inspired by the Go-Go's. Talking about hearing "Our Lips Are Sealed" as a fourteen-year-old, she said, "I've a lot of respect for those ladies: emerging from the LA punk scene and being radical by writing bubblegum pop, which everyone loves somewhere inside."[22]

7
We Haven't Come a Long Way, Baby

To examine *Beauty and the Beat*'s legacy means acknowledging that, sadly, we haven't come a long way, baby. It's been decades since the album was released, but female musicians are still greeted with the same sexism, tired tropes, and gender bias. In a 2015 interview with *Time*, Nicki Minaj summed up the double standard for female musicians: "You never know how much is too much—too much emotion, too much vulnerability, too much power. Everyone wants me to be something different. Women in the industry are judged more. If you speak up for yourself, you're a bitch. If you party too much, you're a whore. Men don't get called these things."[1]

Pop princesses have always existed from Brenda Lee in the 1950s and Marie Osmond in the 1970s to mall rats Debbie Gibson and Tiffany who ruled the 1980s. Used to describe any popular, young female singer, the pop princess era peaked in the late 1990s and early 2000s with the rise of teen singers Britney Spears and Christina Aguilera. There was also Jessica Simpson, Mandy Moore, Hilary Duff, Brandy, Lindsay Lohan (Admit it, "Rumours" was totally fetch.), and countless other young female singers dominating the radio, the celebrity gossip blogs, and MTV's *Total Request Live*.

The term "pop princess" is now used to describe female musicians from Rihanna and Selena Gomez to Ariana Grande and Katy Perry. Like "riot grrrl" in the 1990s, "pop princess" is a reductive term that functions as a catchall for all young female singers, whether they identify with it or not. It fails to acknowledge the diversity of the female musicians it describes, and the use of "princess" implies youth, meaning the pop princess is stuck in a constant state of adolescence, often not permitted to mature beyond the moniker. Britney Spears is often referred to as the original Princess of Pop. "Emerging in the fall of 1998 with '. . . Baby One More Time,' Britney Spears quickly became the princess of pop, helping to usher in a new era for the genre that had gone dormant in the decade that followed New Kids on the Block,"[2] wrote Stacy Lambe in *Rolling Stone*. Spears is the best-selling teen singer of all time and her first two albums, 1999's *. . . Baby One More Time* and 2000's *Oops! . . . I Did It Again*, are counted among the best-selling albums of all time. She has sold nearly 150 million records worldwide, had six number one albums, and five number one singles. She's won MTV awards, *Billboard* awards, and a Grammy. Not bad for someone who was initially rejected by record labels because they wanted female pop groups like TLC and the Spice Girls and boy bands like NSYNC and the Backstreet Boys or because record execs thought "there wasn't going to be another Madonna, another Debbie Gibson, or another Tiffany."[3]

* * *

The theme of the forty-fifth annual American Music Awards in 2017 was "women who take up space." The show featured several female performers, including Pink and Aguilera. It also included a lifetime achievement award for Diana Ross. What didn't it include? A lot of actual female nominees. Of the award's twenty-eight categories, only nine featured women, which seemed odd considering the show's theme. Ladies, we'd like you to take up space, just not in any of the actual categories! Instead of taking home awards, the women were, according to the media, busy fighting. The media was obsessed with a supposed feud between singers Pink and Aguilera. "Did Pink Cringe During Christina Aguilera's AMAs Performance?"[4] asked *Us Weekly*, while stoking the lady feud fire. News outlets from CNN to *People*, along with social media, chimed in with timelines, analysis, and recaps on a feud that had apparently been going on for years. *Vulture* tried to play peacemaker with, "Stop Trying to Make Pink Versus Christina Aguilera Happen (Again)."[5]

Musical mean girls are a narrative pop culture loves to promote, the more shade and side-eye the better. A few months before the American Music Awards, the MTV awards were held. Katy Perry was hosting, and Taylor Swift was premiering a new video. The pre-awards press focused on rehashing the feud between Perry and Swift. Again, there were timelines, *Rolling Stone* explainers like "Katy Perry Vs. Taylor Swift: Pop Stars' Beef History Explained"[6] and more media speculation about a showdown than Perry costume changes during a concert. Miley Cyrus and Nicki Minaj were also attending the show and feuding, in case you were bored with Perry and Swift's bad blood.

Pop culture loves to pit women against each other, especially when it comes to pop princesses. In the early 2000s, the media was obsessed with Britney versus Christina, which played out a lot like Madonna versus Cyndi Lauper in the 1980s. "The Complete History of Christina Aguilera and Britney Spears' Long Running Rivalry—Including Everything You Forgot,"[7] read a 2018 *E! News* headline. Spears was promoted in the press as America's sweetheart (sound familiar?), a wholesome girl next door (sound familiar?), while Aguilera was marketed as a raunchy bad girl. A 1999 *Guardian* piece, describing the two, said, "Christina has a 'naughtier' image than Britney's corn-fed, Midwest, wholesome look."[8] The competitive music industry and a media salivating over every snub, or supposed snub, helped to keep this good girl versus bad-girl feud going for decades.

Spears and Aguilera both grew up in the spotlight. They started singing at an early age and both starred on the *Mickey Mouse Club*, along with Justin Timberlake and Ryan Gosling. Being in show business at a young age, it's only natural their looks and sounds would evolve over time. If we maintained the same look we had when we were teenagers forever, I would be typing this while wearing an acid wash jean jacket, Madonna-inspired fingerless gloves, and a lot of blue Maybelline eye shadow. On the plus side, I would still have my eyebrows cause the overplucking trend of the 1990s hadn't robbed me of them yet.

"There was a shift occurring in both the music and her public image: She was sharper, sexier and singing about more grown-up fare, setting the stage for 2001's *Britney*, which shed her innocent skin and ushered her into adulthood,"[9] wrote

Billboard in 2016 of Spears' change. *Britney* included the single "I'm a Slave 4 U," and the video featured a more mature Spears. The video was voted number one on a MuchMusic, Canada's answer to MTV, list of the fifty sexiest music videos of all time, and Spears' live performance of the song at the 2001 MTV Video Awards, complete with a python on her shoulders, is considered one of the show's best performances. A year later, Aguilera also debuted a sexier, more grown-up look with "Dirrty," the first single off her fourth album 2002's *Stripped.*

For musicians, image changes are not uncommon, but pop princesses feel an added pressure to constantly reinvent themselves. "But it seems that more frequently, female pop artists are not only being pushed to challenge themselves artistically, but to transform everything about themselves with each new release,"[10] read a 2021 *Daily Beast* piece. The article focused on Billie Eilish and Lorde. Specifically, Eilish's transformation to "classic, old-timey pin-up"[11] on the cover of a June 2021 issue of British *Vogue*, as well as a change in sound with her *Happier Than Ever* album, and Lorde embracing a lighter, sunnier side for her third album *Solar Power.* The piece could have easily been referencing any pop princess. "They become chameleons, shedding the current version of themselves, and emerging as a shiny new thing, complete with a different look, aesthetic, and sound,"[12] the piece continued. While it's natural that pop princesses, and chameleons, shed their skin as they age and mature, what's talked about less is how female musicians have been programmed to believe that to stay relevant and sell records they constantly need to change themselves. Male musicians don't face the same level of scrutiny when it comes to their images, nor the same pressure to reinvent those images.

From Lady Gaga and Madonna to Katy Perry and Beyoncé, female pop stars are taught the importance of both the image and the image makeover. Unless you're Courtney Love and then the media doesn't want you to reinvent yourself. They want you forever stuck in 1994. An angry, brash, outspoken, mess, complete with smeared lipstick and a baby doll dress. I am thinking particularly of the skepticism and distrust, on the part of the media, which greeted Love's *The People vs. Larry Flynt* transformation from grieving, grunge widow to Golden Globe-nominated, Versace wearing, Edward Norton dating actress. When a cleaned up, on many levels, Love sat down with Barbara Walters in 1995 for an interview to promote the film, Walters described her as "prom queen meets *Night of the Living Dead*"[13] and a "baby doll gone bad."[14] One of Walters' first questions was, "Ever do drugs in front of your child?"[15] This was right after she asked Love if she was on heroin or any of the other many drugs Walters listed. Female musicians are constantly required to shed their skin, but Love will never be able to leave her celebrity skin behind.

In her 2020 documentary, *Miss Americana*, Taylor Swift talked about how we live in a society "where women in entertainment are discarded in an elephant graveyard at 35."[16] Swift is certainly no stranger to image changes; each album brings us a new Taylor. "Everyone is a shiny new toy for like two years. The female artists have reinvented themselves twenty times more than the male artists. They have to or else you're out of a job. Constantly having to reinvent, constantly finding new facets of yourself that people find to be shiny,"[17] she said. Swift is also an expert at keeping the media and fans guessing at what changes are coming through clues in her videos, her song lyrics, and on her social media accounts. The anticipation of the reinvention being almost as good as the reinvention itself.

When they're not covering her reinvention, the media is busy scrutinizing Swift's song lyrics. She has been criticized for writing excessively about her ex-boyfriends from Jake Gyllenhaal to John Mayer to Joe Jonas in her songs, something that would not be a problem if she was a man. Swift told *Time* magazine in 2014 of the double standards at play when female musicians write about love and relationships:

> You're going to have people who are going to say, "Oh, you know, like, she just writes songs about her ex-boyfriends." And I think frankly that's a very sexist angle to take. No one says that about Ed Sheeran. No one says that about Bruno Mars. They're all writing songs about their exes, their current girlfriends, their love life, and no one raises the red flag there.[18]

Swift has not only been accused of turning her burn book into hit singles but also been accused of not actually writing those singles. The music of female musicians is often attributed to men from the rumors that persist twenty-nine years later that Kurt Cobain wrote Hole's *Live Through This* to the Go-Go's insistence on being filmed playing instruments in their music videos so that people would believe they actually played them on *Beauty and the Beat*. "For a male artist, people instantly assume they write their own music, but for women, they assume it's all manufactured,"[19] singer Dua Lipa told the BBC. If a female musician is successful there must have been a man behind her, and people really, really want to hear about that man. "You will also notice of the big successful female artists, there is always a 'man behind the woman' piece. If it's Beyoncé, it's Jay-Z. If it's Adele, it's Paul Epworth. Me? It was Mark Ronson and the same with Amy Winehouse. You never get that with men,"[20] said Lily Allen in a 2014 piece in *NME*. Female musicians are often granted legitimacy based on their proximity to male musicians. One of the best examples of this is when *Pitchfork* decided to finally review Taylor Swift's *1989* album, but only after singer Ryan Adams had recorded an all-covers version of it. "Sure enough, even though Swift is the biggest artist in music, and has been going multi-platinum for almost a decade, it took a guy's acoustic covers for one of the most successful and influential music sites on the Web to finally deem an album of her songs worthy of one of its 25 reviews per week,"[21] wrote Forrest Wickman in *Slate*.

Just like the Go-Go's, female musicians are still asked sexist questions about what it's like to be a girl playing music or a girl playing in a band. They are asked invasive and inappropriate questions about their personal lives or trivial questions about their appearance and fashion. When a German radio show host asked Swift when she was going to settle down and have kids she responded, "I really do not think men are asked that question when they turn 30, so I'm not going to answer that now."[22] Rihanna was asked on a red carpet what she was looking for in a man to which the singer replied that she wasn't looking for a man at all. In a 2015 Los

Angeles radio interview, Ariana Grande was asked if she had to choose between makeup or her phone, which she would pick. Grande shot down the journalists for assuming those are the only things that women cared about. Tabloid journalism, celebrity gossip blogs, and social media have increasingly blurred the line between a star's personal life and their professional life. We know our favorite stars more than we did in the pre-TMZ days, which can make journalists feel like these personal questions are acceptable, but the entitlement of journalists seems especially pronounced when it comes to young, female musicians. They feel singers like Swift owe them unlimited access, like their whole lives should be laid bare to be picked apart week after week in the pages of *In Touch* or on Twitter.

There are many disturbing moments in the 2021 *New York Times* documentary *Framing Britney Spears*. A review of the film in the *Guardian* read:

> This was a well-curated assemblage of interview footage and commentary from people there at the time—one who had worked with most big boybands noted that not one of their members was ever scrutinised to anything like the degree Spears was. It comprehensively showcased the overt and systemic misogyny Spears (and by extension any young, female performer) faced and faces, within the industry as well as beyond.[23]

Some of the hardest scenes to watch involved male reporters asking a young Spears about her breasts and her virginity. Journalists felt entitled to ask Spears intensely personal questions, even when she looked extremely uncomfortable and nervously tried to deflect their questions with laughter. While it was largely male journalists who made Spears uncomfortable, female journalists were also less than sympathetic to the pop singer. The documentary featured a clip from ABC's *Primetime* of journalist Diane Sawyer asking Spears personal questions about her breakup with Justin Timberlake and blaming Spears for hurting him. She also asked Spears about parents' concerns that the singer was a bad influence on her young fans. Spears eventually requested a break from the interview while wiping away tears. Way to be an ally, Diane.

Spears bore all the blame for the breakup with Timberlake, and the media never let her forget it. He not only bragged about taking her virginity on a Los Angeles morning radio show, but was hailed a hero for doing so. "Can we ever forgive Justin Timberlake for all that sissy music? Hey . . . at least he got into Britney's pants,"[24] read a 2002 *Details* magazine coverline. The media's obsession in the early aughts with purity culture and Spears' virginity was not only misogynistic and deeply inappropriate but also tied Spears' worth to her virginity and robbed her of agency over her sexuality. Spears was vilified for supposedly cheating on Timberlake, a narrative he helped to fuel with his "Cry Me a River" video, which featured him getting revenge on a Spears lookalike. When he was done with his Spears' blame game, he moved on to Janet Jackson. Timberlake refused to take responsibility for what happened at the 2004 Super Bowl halftime show and forced Jackson to deal with the fallout, which saw her disinvited from the Grammys and radio stations stopped playing her songs. Her post Super Bowl album, *Damita Jo*, didn't have the same success as previous releases and when Jackson appeared on television some stations added a five-second delay in case she ripped her top off in the middle of David Letterman's show. Meanwhile, Timberlake was busy bringing sexy back.

* * *

The tales of sexual assault and harassment young female singers have endured are far too many to list here. One of the most high-profile recent examples was Kesha's 2014 lawsuit against Dr. Luke, the singer's former producer and head of the record label she is currently signed to Kemosabe Records. Kesha has accused Dr. Luke of sexual, emotional, and physical abuse and has demanded she be released from her contract. He sued her for defamation and a series of suits and counter-suits have been before the courts since 2014. Other female singers, including Lady Gaga, Kelly Clarkson, and Taylor Swift, have expressed support for Kesha in her ongoing legal battles with the producer. In 2017, Swift won a civil suit against an ex-DJ she said grabbed her ass at a 2013 meet and greet in Denver. Haim has called out predatory behavior and pay inequality in the industry. "I had an experience when we were first getting signed, and we were doing showcases for labels. After the performance, I was just talking to an A&R, just a normal conversation. Out of nowhere really, he just looks at me and goes, 'So tell me the truth, do you make the same faces on stage that you make in bed?'"[25] Este Haim told *Teen Vogue* in 2018. Singer Demi Lovato's new single "29" contained lyrics that seemed to allude to the twelve-year age gap in the singer's previous relationship with actor Wilmer Valderrama, which started when Lovato was just eighteen.

* * *

No pop princess has been judged more harshly for her behavior than Spears. The infamous paparazzi photo of Spears, Lindsay Lohan, and Paris Hilton piled into the front seat of a car outside the Beverly Hills Hotel in 2006 was one of the defining images of the 2000s. The *New York Post* ran it with the headline, "Bimbo Summit." Stay classy, *New York Post*. The photo perfectly captured the mood of the time, when pop culture was obsessed with rich, young people, especially women, from Lauren Conrad on *The Hills* to Marissa Cooper on *The O.C.* to Blair Waldorf on *Gossip Girl* and Nicole Richie on the cover of *Us Weekly* week after week.

It was a difficult time for Spears who was clearly dealing with mental health issues that were sensationalized and treated like nothing more than a punch line by the media. Hearing a paparazzo in *Framing Britney Spears* refer to shots of Spears having a meltdown as a "money shot,"[26] perfectly summed up the media's level of understanding and sensitivity when it came to Spears' mental health. The same photographer said that if Spears wanted the paparazzi to stop hounding her, she should just ask them to, like it was her responsibility to stop their predatory behavior and like that would have worked at all. "It seems almost too obvious to point out that this wouldn't have happened if Spears were male. Famous men, who suffer mental breakdowns, simply are not controlled in the same way. Just as the patriarchy has helped Jamie Spears assert control over his daughter, it has also worked to prevent similar fates for men,"[27] wrote Ella Alexander in *Harper's Bazaar*. There's a distinct gender bias when it comes to celebrity meltdowns; we have seen this not only with Spears but in the coverage of countless young women from Lovato's addiction and mental health to Lohan's struggles over the years.

In her 2015 acceptance speech for Woman of the Year, at *Billboard's* Women in Music event, Lady Gaga said, "But what I really want to say is that it is really hard sometimes for women in music. It's like a fuckin' boys club that we just can't get into."[28] Unfortunately, not everyone would agree. At the 2018 Grammys, Neil Portnow, president of the Recording Academy, said that if women want to get ahead in the music industry they need to "step up."[29] For Portnow, it's women's responsibility to fix the problems in the industry. His comments did not go over well. "Women in music don't need to 'step up'—women have been stepping up since the beginning of time. Stepping up, and also stepping aside,"[30] said Pink, who took a moment away from her years-long feud with Aguilera to respond.

Stats definitely support the boy's club claim. A 2020 study found that less than thirteen percent of songwriters were women and less than three percent were producers. According to a 2021 survey, sixty-four percent of respondents said harassment and objectification were a barrier to their participation in the music industry.[31] Music algorithms also regularly recommend male artists over female artists, as a 2021 study found. In an analysis of over 300,000 users' listening behavior over a nine-year period, the study found that only twenty-five percent of the artists listened to were female. "When we tested the algorithm we found, on average, the first recommended track was by a man, along with the next six. Users had to wait until song seven or eight to hear one by a woman,"[32] said the study. Summer means festival season which each year brings a new onslaught of pieces about the lack of female representation at music festivals. They have become a staple of festivals, like overpriced bottled water and long porta potty lineups. There is also what writer Anwen Crawford described in the *New Yorker* as, "The record store, the guitar shop, and now social media: when it comes to popular music, these places become stages for the display of male prowess."[33] Crawford is also the author of the excellent book in this series on Hole's *Live Through This*. I've experienced the stages Crawford described many, many, many times in my life. I recently told a man I was a Nirvana fan and after telling me he thought that was "cute" he spent the next twenty minutes quizzing me and asking me if I was familiar with any albums by the band besides *Nevermind*, which he let me know was "super popular when it came out." I wanted to find a copy of *Nevermind* and drag it slowly across my throat to make the pain stop.

Conclusion
They Still Got the Beat

On Saturday October 30, 2021, the Go-Go's were inducted into the Rock & Roll Hall of Fame, forty years after *Beauty and the Beat* was released and fifteen years after the band was eligible. "Better late than never and beyond well-deserved,"[1] Sleater-Kinney's Carrie Brownstein said of the band's induction. The class of 2021 also included Foo Fighters, Carole King, Tina Turner, and Jay-Z. Lifelong Go-Go's fan, actress Drew Barrymore inducted the band with a touching and heartfelt speech about the impact they had on her. "The Go-Go's had been in my personal hall of fame since I was six years old,"[2] she said. In a 2012 issue of *V Magazine*, Barrymore talked about discovering the band for the first time. "I went out and bought their album *Beauty and the Beat*, and as the vinyl twirled, my whole world changed. I stared at the girls on the cover like they were a gateway to cool. The fact that they were girls made me feel not only invited but more important— like I could be a badass too."[3] Referring to the band as her "heroes," in her induction speech she talked about how *Beauty and the Beat* was the first album she bought. Me too, Drew. "*Beauty and the Beat* blew the doors of my life off," Barrymore said. "It sounded like pure possibility."[4]

Her speech also included Barrymore recreating the iconic *Beauty and the Beat* album cover by dressing up in a white bath towel and face mask. A cover she described as "the coolest girls in the world taking a spa day in cool girl heaven."[5] During the induction, Green Day's Billie Joe Armstrong talked about how the Go-Go's wrote some of the best songs ever while Sleater-Kinney members Corin Tucker and Brownstein talked about the band's legacy. "They were fuelled by a 'we don't take no for an answer' attitude,"[6] said Susanna Hoffs of the Bangles. "They changed my life. They made me believe that things were possible,"[7] said Barrymore of the Go-Go's. Me too, Drew. In a statement the band released when they received news of their induction they said, "Women have always been a vital part of the ever-changing music business and The Go-Go's are so proud to have our success story honored and recognized by fans and voters."[8]

At the ceremony, the band performed "Vacation," "Our Lips Are Sealed," and "We Got the Beat." All five members took a turn at the microphone to give thanks. "The Go-Go's will be advocating for the inclusion of more women,"[9] Valentine said in her portion of the band's acceptance speech, referencing the Rock & Roll Hall of Fame. In a 2019 piece for *Billboard*, music writer and journalist Evelyn McDonnell talked about the gender imbalance in inductees.

Since the Hall started inducting artists in 1986, when zero of the 16 inaugural inductees were women, until the Oct.

15 announcement of the 2020 nominees (72 individuals, three of whom are female), women have been egregiously underrepresented. My research assistants and I have been crunching the numbers and the results are alarming: Only 7.7 percent of all individuals inducted into the Hall have been female, and 4.17% of this year's nominees are women.[10]

There's also a racial imbalance among nominees, according to McDonnell. "The percentage of total people of color in the hall has declined every year from an impressive high of 55.8% in 1989 to the current low of 32.7%. Only 13 nominees, or 18.6%, of this year's nominees are black, Latinx, Native American or Asian."[11]

The first woman inducted into the Rock & Roll Hall of Fame was Aretha Franklin in 1987. At the end of her induction acceptance speech in 2019, Janet Jackson said, "Rock and Roll Hall of Fame, please: 2020, induct more women."[12] Nirvana was inducted by R.E.M.'s Michael Stipe in 2014, the first year the band was eligible, and band members Dave Grohl and Krist Novoselic chose women, including Joan Jett, Lorde, Annie Clark, and Kim Gordon, to sing Cobain's songs during the ceremony's live performance. The band's induction coincided with the twentieth anniversary of Cobain's death, and they wanted the performance to be a celebration of the singer, rather than a eulogy. "We thought, 'Wait it has to be all women,'" Grohl said. "'Don't even ask anyone else. If we can fill the Rock and Roll Hall of Fame performance with these incredible women singing Nirvana songs, then we'll have achieved our own revolution.' It also added a whole other dimension to the show. It added substance and depth, so it didn't turn into a eulogy. It was more about the future."[13]

The Go-Go's induction was also monumental because the band was the first from the Los Angeles punk scene to be inducted, prompting a text from X's John Doe to Wiedlin that said, "OG punks for the win!"[14] The Go-Go's credit Ellwood's documentary and the Rock & Roll Hall of Fame induction with helping to increase awareness of the band and its legacy. "Once we got nominated [for The Rock & Roll Hall of Fame] and the documentary came out, and people wrote that we were a real band that came from the streets and were self-made, that's when the narrative changed," Valentine told *Bust* magazine. "It changed once that became the story, instead of 'Aren't they cute and bubbly?' Aren't they the girl next door?'"[15] Schock agreed, "Our story had gotten overshadowed by, 'Oh, they were crazy. They were wild. They got high. They broke up.' So what? All bands do that stuff,"[16] she told *Rolling Stone*. The induction and the documentary told the Go-Go's story as it should be told, rather than the *Behind the Music* style treatment that sensationalized parts of the band's story. If you haven't seen Ellwood's documentary, it's worth a watch or ten. Finish reading this book first though, you've only got a few pages left.

A few months after the induction Barrymore turned forty-seven. On February 22, 2022, the Go-Go's surprised Barrymore, via video, on her talk show to wish her a Happy Birthday. The band had a special birthday present for Barrymore. They awarded her the honorary title of "sixth Go-Go" and presented her with a copy of *Beauty and the Beat* with Barrymore photoshopped onto the cover, towel, and face mask included. Genuinely touched, Barrymore cried and thanked her heroes for giving her "permission to dream and think big."[17] Me too, Drew.

* * *

The band's induction into the Rock & Roll Hall of Fame came forty-three years after the Go-Go's first formed. Their second album *Vacation* was released in 1982 and, while it didn't sell as well as *Beauty and the Beat*, it featured the top forty hit song "Vacation," which went to number eight on the charts. The video featured the girls waterskiing in tiaras and pink tutus. The band passed the time on set drinking, smoking, and wandering the streets of Los Angeles in their tutus. If you watch the video closely you can see they're a little wobbly on their skis toward the end of it. In 1984, they released *Talk Show*, their third album, which included the songs "Head over Heels" and "Turn to You." It would be their last album for a while. The Go-Go's broke up in 1985. There were creative differences, tensions among band members, and issues over things like songwriting royalties. It also just wasn't as much fun anymore. Wiedlin has talked about band members screaming at each other backstage and then minutes later having to plaster a smile on to perform for thousands of screaming fans. She called it "robo go-going." Wiedlin was the first to quit in October 1984 over publishing royalties and a band dynamic that saw her request to sing a song she had written on *Talk Show* denied. Paula Jean Brown was hired as a bassist and Valentine moved to rhythm guitar to replace Wiedlin. The new lineup played Rock in Rio in 1985, but in May 1985 Carlisle and Caffey decided to disband the group, a decision that apparently blindsided Schock and Valentine. Band members went on to solo careers, the most successful being Carlisle. There were some lawsuits along the way and stretches of time where band members didn't talk.

In 1994, they released the retrospective *Return to the Valley of the Go-Go's*, featuring three new recordings. The band got back together several times starting in the 1990s to play shows, tour, and release their fourth album *God Bless the Go-Go's* in 2001. The Go-Go's did a farewell tour in 2016, but thankfully, goodbye wasn't forever and the band still performs together. In 2011, the Go-Go's "Ladies Gone Wild" tour celebrated the thirtieth anniversary of *Beauty and the Beat*. One of the highlights of Ellwood's documentary was seeing the band working together on a new song. On July 31, 2020, the band released "Club Zero," their first new song in nineteen years, and the band has toured since then with some dates rescheduled due to the Covid-19 pandemic. My hope is that the Go-Go's will be coming soon to a town near me.

*   *   *

I was happy when the Go-Go's were inducted into the Rock & Roll Hall of Fame, but I was also angry that it had taken so long. "We were the first of our kind,"[18] said Carlisle. "We're kind of American icons, in that we represent girls being in control and trying to get ahead without compromising. It's more than music. A lot of people think of us as a band that had a lot of balls."[19] She's right.

While researching this book, I was struck by how little the gender bias experienced by female musicians has changed. At times, it was depressing to look at the lack of progress that has been made since the Go-Go's started in 1978. Chapter 7 was, to put it mildly, kind of a bummer to research when I looked at how pop princesses are treated and how little has changed for young female musicians. I was telling a friend the story about the Go-Go's touring the UK in 1980 with Madness and the Specials when audience members greeted the band with, "show me your tits." My friend said, "that's awful, but that kind of stuff doesn't happen anymore. No one would do that now to a female band." I admired my friend's optimism. A few days later I watched *Trainwreck: Woodstock '99*, one of two recent documentaries about the music festival. One of my favorite things about Woodstock 1999 docs is that they often start with the question: "How could things go so horribly wrong?" and then in the first five minutes show you ten extremely obvious reasons for how things could go so horribly wrong from corporate greed to Fred Durst to an all-night rave tent. There's a scene early in the documentary where audience members (So many cargo shorts. So many backward baseball caps.) yell "show me your tits"[20] at singer Sheryl Crow, one of few female performers on the bill, who tried to laugh it off as best she could. I didn't have the heart to tell my optimistic friend what happened to Crow. I would also like to point out, in case you are planning a music festival, that handing out candles to the crowd and then asking Anthony Kiedis of the Red Hot Chili Peppers, which were the final band that played, if he could help you calm the crowd down is a very, very bad idea. If you have read his memoir *Scar Tissue*, you know he has impulse control problems and really shouldn't be your fire marshal.

I wanted to end this book on a hopeful note. I wanted to be able to say that things are getting better and will get better for female musicians. There are reasons to be hopeful. I am inspired by initiatives like NPR's *Turning the Tables* series, which started from a desire to challenge the sexism of the pop music canon. The series, co-founded by NPR music critic Ann Powers and editor Marissa Lorusso, began in 2017 and has included essays, podcasts, and a list of the 150 greatest albums by women. Powers described the list as "the beginning of new conversation."[21] A conversation that was necessary and long overdue. "One is still needed when it comes to women's place in music history, despite decades of efforts by feminist historians, critics, activists and musicians themselves. For the past half-century—the period that this list roughly covers—most mainstream musical 'best' lists feature startlingly few women, especially in their top ranks,"[22] she said in 2017. *Pitchfork* has been revisiting the works of female musicians and there are fewer of the Women in Music special issues that were so prevalent in the 1990s and served to marginalize women, rather than celebrate them. You get one issue a year, ladies, that's it! Podcasts like the popular *You're Wrong About* and documentaries like *Framing Britney Spears* provide us with the opportunity to rewrite and revisit the history for female celebrities and musicians.

With this conclusion, I wanted to recapture that hope I felt when I first heard *Beauty and the Beat*. When the world was filled with possibilities, for me, for Drew, and for countless other young girls. "We just happen to be five girls who got together and made some music and had a great time. The fact that we were women was secondary. All these years later, there still isn't a band like The Go-Go's,"[23] Schock told *USA Today* in 2021. It's true there isn't.

So, one last time, the Go-Go's were the first and only all-female band who wrote their own songs and played their own instruments to have a number one record. Tell your friends. Scream it from the rooftops. Everyone should know.

Acknowledgments

Thank you to Leah Babb-Rosenfeld, Rachel Moore, and everyone at Bloomsbury. Thank you to Sarah Piña for your great edits, guidance, and kind words. Also, my apologies to the couple in front of me at the coffee shop who had "holy shit!" yelled very loudly in their ears after I received Leah's email letting me know my proposal had been accepted. To say I was excited would be an understatement.

Thank you to my *This Magazine* family and especially Lauren McKeon, who I was lucky enough to have as a work wife for many years. Thank you, Lauren, for encouraging me to write about pop culture and giving me the confidence to do so.

Thank you to Krista Stevens at *Longreads* for accepting a piece about Courtney Love that would start me thinking about the gender bias that female musicians experience. Thank you also for always letting me keep the puns. It is a pleasure working with you.

I think of the Go-Go's as a musical girl gang, and I am very lucky to have my own girl gang. Thank you to Joyce Byrne and Sue Carter for being members of that gang and for all the love, support, encouragement, cat photos, and dance parties that would make the Go-Go's proud. I am very lucky to have you both in my life.

A big, big thank you to my family and especially my Mom. Thank you Mom for everything. For your guidance, your love, your support, and for being the best cheerleader a kid could ask for. Thank you also for giving me the allowance money that I would use to buy *Beauty and the Beat*.

Thank you to my cat Feline Bureau of Investigation Special Agent Dale Cooper (aka Cooper), who sat patiently beside my laptop while I worked on this book.

Last, but not least, thank you to Belinda, Jane, Charlotte, Gina, and Kathy. You changed my life, and I can never thank you enough for that.

Notes

Introduction

1 Steve Pond, "The Go-Go's: Ladies First," *Rolling Stone*, August 5, 1982, https://www.rollingstone.com/music/music-news/the-go-gos-ladies-first-89680/.

2 Pond, "The Go-Go's."

3 *Behind the Music*, "The Go-Go's," YouTube, 43:19, April 23, 2018.

4 Keaton Bell, "How the Go-Go's Found Their Beat: An Oral History," *Vogue*, August 4, 2020, https://www.vogue.com/article/go-gos-40th-anniversary-beauty-and-the-beat-oral-history-belinda-carlisle.

5 Hilary Hughes, "How The Go-Go's Perfected Pop-Punk," NPR, August 5, 2020, https://www.gpb.org/news/2020/08/05/how-the-go-gos-perfected-pop-punk.

6 Gerri Hirshey, *We Gotta Get Out of This Place: The True, Tough Story of Women in Rock* (New York: Grove Press, 2002), 125.

7 Alison Ellwood, *The Go-Go's* (SHOWTIME, 2020), 1:38.

8 Sandra L. Stricklin, "The Fine Art of Fun—A Big Part of the Go-Go's Success Story," *The Christian Science Monitor*, May 18, 1982, https://www.csmonitor.com/layout/set/amphtml/1982/0518/051801.html.

Chapter 1

1   Alison Ellwood, *The Go-Go's* (SHOWTIME, 2020), 1:38.

2   Alice Bag (host), "We Were There: Voices from L.A. Punk's First Wave: An Oral History," *Razorcake*, #79, April/May 2014, https://razorcake.org/we-were-there-voices-from-l-a-punks-first-wave-an-oral-history-hosted-by-alice-bag/.

3   Belinda Carlisle, *Lips Unsealed* (New York: Crown Publishers, 2010), 49.

4   Sylvie Simmons, "The Go-Go's: Ready Steady Go-Go's," *Sounds* (1980). The Go-Go's. Rock's Backpages. Accessed August 15, 2022. http://www.rocksbackpages.com/Library/Article/the-go-gos-ready-steady-go-gos.

5   Ellwood, *The Go-Go's.*

6   Quinn Moreland, "*Beauty and the Beat* The Go-Go's," *Pitchfork*, October 20, 2019, https://pitchfork.com/reviews/albums/the-go-gos-beauty-and-the-beat/.

7   Moreland, "*Beauty and the Beat.*"

8   Hilary Hughes, "How The Go-Go's Perfected Pop-Punk," NPR, August 5, 2020, https://www.gpb.org/news/2020/08/05/how-the-go-gos-perfected-pop-punk.

9   *Behind the Music*, "The Go-Go's," YouTube, 43:19, April 23, 2018.

10   Rob Tannenbaum, "The Go-Go's Recall the Debauched Days of Their Hit 'We Got the Beat' 35 Years Later," *Billboard*, May 20, 2016, https://www.billboard.com/music/pop/the-go-gos-we-got-the-beat-35th-anniversary-interview-billboard-music-awards-7378161/.

11   Elizabeth Sankey, "From Punk Rock to Sugar Pop: Tracing the Music and Style of the Go-Go's," *Vice*, September 23, 2014,

https://www.vice.com/en/article/ryy9kr/from-punk-rock-to-sugar-pop-tracing-the-music-and-style-of-the-go-gos.

12 "Staged Events," *Slash Magazine*, September 1978.

13 "Staged Events," *Slash Magazine*, September 1978.

14 Tannenbaum, "The Go-Go's Recall the Debauched Days of Their Hit 'We Got the Beat' 35 Years Later."

15 Kathy Valentine, *All I Ever Wanted* (Austin: University of Texas Press, 2020), 99.

16 Mike Stand, "Go-Go's," *Smash Hits* (1982). The Go-Go's. Rock's Backpages. Accessed August 15, 2022. http://www.rocksbackpages.com/Library/Article/go-gos.

17 Tannenbaum, "The Go-Go's Recall the Debauched Days of Their Hit 'We Got the Beat' 35 Years Later."

18 Don Snowden, "The Go-Gos Go!!," *New York Rocker* (1980). The Go-Go's. Rock's Backpages. Accessed July 13, 2022. http://www.rocksbackpages.com/Library/Article/the-go-gos-go.

19 Snowden, "The Go-Gos Go!!," *New York Rocker* (1980).

20 "Go-Go's," *Slash Magazine*, January 1979.

21 Snowden, "The Go-Gos Go!!," *New York Rocker* (1980).

22 Carl Wiser, "Jane Wiedlin of the Go-Go's," *Songfacts* (2007). The Go-Go's, Jane Wiedlin. Rock's Backpages. Accessed July 13, 2022. http://www.rocksbackpages.com/Library/Article/jane-wiedlin-of-the-go-gos.

23 Ellwood, *The Go-Go's*.

24 Jane Lupo, "Go-Go's," *Trouser Press*, 1981, https://www.gogos.com/2011/06/25/from-the-vault-trouser-press-1981/.

25 Lyndsey Parker, "The Go-Go's Talk Partying Past, Hall of Fame Snub and 'Emotional' Documentary," *Yahoo Music*,

July 29, 2020, https://ca.sports.yahoo.com/news/the-go
-gos-talk-partying-past-hall-of-fame-snub-and-emotional
-documentary-you-cant-deny-what-weve-done-221531086
.html.

26 Lupo, "Go-Go's."

27 Hughes, "How The Go-Go's Perfected Pop-Punk."

Chapter 2

1 Gillian G. Gaar, *She's A Rebel: The History of Women in Rock & Roll* (New York: Seal Press, 1992), 32.

2 Gaar, *She's A Rebel*, 32.

3 *Slash Magazine*, Vol 3. No. 5.

4 The Go-Go's, "Bio." Accessed June 10, 2022, https://www
.gogos.com/bio/.

5 Jason Cherkis, "The Lost Girls," *The Huffington Post Highline*, July 2015, https://highline.huffingtonpost.com/articles/en/the
-lost-girls/.

6 Cherkis, "The Lost Girls."

7 Cherkis, "The Lost Girls."

8 Cherkis, "The Lost Girls."

9 Cherie Currie, *Neon Angel: A Memoir of a Runaway* (New York: HarperCollins, 2010), 86.

10 Cherkis, "The Lost Girls."

11 Geoff Barton, "Fanny: The Untold Story of the original Queens of Noise," *Classic Rock* (2015). Fanny. Rock's Backpages. Accessed July 13, 2022. http://www

.rocksbackpages.com/Library/Article/fanny-the-untold-story
-of-the-original-queens-of-noise.

12   Barton, "Fanny."

13   Barton, "Fanny."

14   Barton, "Fanny."

15   Kathleen Johnson, "Fanny's June Millington: Grrrl Power's
     First Flash in Rock," *Vintage Guitar*. Accessed August 1,
     2022. https://www.vintageguitar.com/27947/fannys-june
     -millington/.

16   Rhian E. Jones, "Post-Punk: Raw, Female Sound," in *Women
     Make Noise: Girl Bands from Motown to the Modern*, ed. Julia
     Downes (Twickenham: Supernova Books, 2012), 193.

17   William E. Badgley, *Here to Be Heard: The Story of the Slits*
     (Head Gear Films, 2017), 1:26.

18   Badgley, *Here to Be Heard: The Story of the Slits*.

19   Jones, "Post-Punk: Raw, Female Sound," 200.

20   Badgley, *Here to Be Heard: The Story of the Slits*.

21   Badgley, *Here to Be Heard: The Story of the Slits*.

Chapter 3

1   Rob Tannenbaum, "The Go-Go's Recall the Debauched Days
    of Their Hit 'We Got the Beat' 35 Years Later," *Billboard*, May
    20, 2016, https://www.billboard.com/music/pop/the-go-gos
    -we-got-the-beat-35th-anniversary-interview-billboard-music
    -awards-7378161/.

2   Tannenbaum, "The Go-Go's."

3   Tannenbaum, "The Go-Go's."

4   Don Snowden, "The Go-Gos Go!!," *New York Rocker* (1980).
    The Go-Go's. Rock's Backpages. Accessed July 13, 2022. http://
    www.rocksbackpages.com/Library/Article/the-go-gos-go.

5   Hilary Hughes, "How The Go-Go's Perfected Pop-Punk," NPR,
    August 5, 2020, https://www.gpb.org/news/2020/08/05/how
    -the-go-gos-perfected-pop-punk.

6   Quinn Moreland, "*Beauty and the Beat*: The Go-Go's," *Pitchfork*,
    October 20, 2019, https://pitchfork.com/reviews/albums/the-go
    -gos-beauty-and-the-beat/.

7   Toby Goldstein, "The Go-Go's: *Beauty and the Beat* (IRS),"
    Musician (1981). The Go-Go's. Rock's Backpages. Accessed
    August 1, 2022. http://www.rocksbackpages.com/Library/
    Article/the-go-gos-ibeauty-and-the-beati-irs.

8   Carl Wiser, "Jane Wiedlin of the Go-Go's," *Songfacts* (2007).
    The Go-Go's, Jane Wiedlin. Rock's Backpages. Accessed July
    13, 2022. http://www.rocksbackpages.com/Library/Article/jane
    -wiedlin-of-the-go-gos.

9   Audrey Golden, "The Go-Go's *Beauty and the Beat*: A 40th
    Anniversary Celebration," *Louder than War*, July 8, 2021,
    https://louderthanwar.com/the-go-gos-beauty-and-the-beat-a
    -40th-anniversary-celebration/.

Chapter 4

1   Steve Pond, "The Go-Go's: Ladies First," *Rolling Stone*, August
    5, 1982, https://www.rollingstone.com/music/music-news/the
    -go-gos-ladies-first-89680/.

2   Mark Cooper, "The Go-Go's: I-Beam, San Francisco CA,"
    Record Mirror (1980). The Go-Go's. Rock's Backpages.

Accessed July 13, 2022. http://www.rocksbackpages.com/ Library/Article/the-go-gos-i-beam-san-francisco-ca.

3   Cooper, "The Go-Go's: I-Beam, San Francisco CA."

4   Audrey Golden, "The Go-Go's *Beauty and the Beat*: A 40th Anniversary Celebration," *Louder Than War*, July 8, 2021, https://louderthanwar.com/the-go-gos-beauty-and-the-beat-a -40th-anniversary-celebration/.

5   Toby Goldstein, "They Think They're Go-Go," *Creem* (1981). The Go-Go's. Rock's Backpages. Accessed July 13, 2022. http:// www.rocksbackpages.com/Library/Article/they-think-theyre -go-go.

6   Goldstein, "They Think They're Go-Go."

7   Rick Johnson, "The Runaways," *Creem*, April 1977.

8   Keaton Bell, "How the Go-Go's Found Their Beat: An Oral History," *Vogue*, August 4, 2020, https://www.vogue.com/ article/go-gos-40th-anniversary-beauty-and-the-beat-oral -history-belinda-carlisle.

9   Kathy Valentine, *All I Ever Wanted* (Texas: University of Texas Press, 2020), 164.

10   Quinn Moreland, "*Beauty and the Beat* The Go-Go's," *Pitchfork*, October 20, 2019, https://pitchfork.com/reviews/ albums/the-go-gos-beauty-and-the-beat/.

11   *People Magazine*, 1981, https://www.gogos.com/2011/05/17/ from-the-vault-people-magazine/.

12   Pond, "The Go-Go's"

13   Pond, "The Go-Go's."

14   Julie Panebianco, "Hey Hey! We're the Go-Go's!," *Boston Rock* (1981). The Go-Go's, The Specials. Rock's Backpages. Accessed

August 2, 2022. http://www.rocksbackpages.com/Library/Article/hey-hey-were-the-go-gos.

15 Richard Harrington, "The Go-Go's Go Get 'Em," *The Washington Post*, September 19, 1982, https://www.washingtonpost.com/archive/lifestyle/style/1982/09/19/the-go-gos-go-get-em/46b2f76b-aa0c-4549-a70e-f266a451180f/.

16 Panebianco, "Hey Hey! We're the Go-Go's!."

17 Tracy Moore, "There's More to *The Go-Go's* Than Peppy Hits," *Vanity Fair*, August 3, 2020, https://www.vanityfair.com/hollywood/2020/08/the-go-gos-documentary-music-showtime.

18 *Behind the Music*, "The Go-Go's," YouTube, 43:19, April 23, 2018.

19 Charlotte Caffey, interview by Talia Schlanger, "Q," CBC, August 24, 2020, https://www.cbc.ca/radio/q/monday-aug-24-2020-charlotte-caffey-danny-devito-and-more-1.5695517.

20 Paul Elliott, "The Go-Go's: The Fab Femme Five," *Q* (2002). The Go-Go's. Rock's Backpages. Accessed July 13, 2022. http://www.rocksbackpages.com/Library/Article/the-go-gos-the-fab-femme-five.

21 Asif Kapadia, *Amy* (James Gay-Rees, 2015), 2:16.

22 Kapadia, *Amy*.

23 Kapadia, *Amy*.

24 Kapadia, *Amy*.

25 Atte Oksanen, "Female Rock Stars and Addiction in Autobiographies," *Nordic Studies on Alcohol and Drugs* 30 (November 2012): 136, https://journals.sagepub.com/doi/pdf/10.2478/nsad-2013-0009.

26 Hilary Hughes, "How The Go-Go's Perfected Pop-Punk," NPR, August 5, 2020, https://www.gpb.org/news/2020/08/05/how-the-go-gos-perfected-pop-punk.

27 Misty Harris, "Female Artists 'Hypersexualized' by *Rolling Stone*: Study," *Windsor Star*, July 26, 2011, https://windsorstar.com/news/female-artists-hypersexualized-by-rolling-stone-study.

28 Tavi Gevinson, "Britney Spears Was Never in Control," *The Cut*, February 23, 2021, https://www.thecut.com/2021/02/tavi-gevinson-britney-spears-was-never-in-control.html.

29 Gevinson, "Britney Spears Was Never in Control."

30 Jessica Hopper, "'It Was Us Against Those Guys': The Women Who Transformed *Rolling Stone* in the Mid-70s," *Vanity Fair*, August 28, 2018, https://www.vanityfair.com/style/2018/08/the-women-who-transformed-rolling-stone-in-the-mid-70s.

Chapter 5

1 Jonathan Cohen, "Pat Benatar Drops 'Hit Me with Your Best Shot' After Spate of Gun Violence," *Spin*, July 22, 2022, https://www.spin.com/2022/07/pat-benatar-drops-hit-me-with-your-best-shot-after-spate-of-gun-violence/.

2 Pat Benatar, *Between a Heart and a Rock Place* (New York: HarperCollins, 2010), 89.

3 Debbie Harry, *Face It* (New York: Dey Street Books, 2019), 129.

4 Benatar, *Between a Heart and a Rock Place*, 135.

5 Benatar, *Between a Heart and a Rock Place*.

6 Gillian G. Gaar, "'80s Darlings The Go-Go's Prove They've Still Got the Beat," *Goldmine*, November 28, 2011, https://www

.goldminemag.com/articles/80s-darlings-the-go-gos-prove
-theyve-still-got-the-beat.

7 Gaar, "'80s Darlings The Go-Go's Prove They've Still Got the
   Beat."

8 John Walters, "How the Retiring Go-Go's Became the Ideal
   Soundtrack to Suburban Teen rebellion," *Newsweek*, August
   30, 2016, https://www.newsweek.com/go-gos-play-their-final
   -show-l-tracing-how-they-became-ideal-soundtrack-494589.

9 Walters, "How the Retiring Go-Go's Became the Ideal
   Soundtrack to Suburban Teen Rebellion."

10 J. D. Considine, "Go-Go's Girl Talk Is Tops," *Washington
    Post*, July 6, 1984, https://www.washingtonpost.com/archive/
    lifestyle/1984/07/06/go-gos-girl-talk-is-tops/8b8685d7-8a0e
    -4745-9598-fa2f061fb8ca/.

11 Lori Majewski and Jonathan Bernstein, *Mad World: An Oral
    History of New Wave Artists and Songs That Defined the 1980s*
    (Abrams: New York, 2014), 12.

12 Alison Ellwood, *The Go-Go's* (SHOWTIME, 2020), 1:38.

13 Craig Marks, "Forty Years Ago, MTV Changed Music Forever.
    These Four Rock Icons Remember All Too Well," *Los Angeles
    Times*, July 28, 2021, https://www.latimes.com/entertainment
    -arts/music/story/2021-07-28/mtv-40th-anniversary-billy
    -idol-go-gos-huey-lewis-reo-speedwagon.

14 Marks, "Forty Years Ago, MTV Changed Music Forever. These
    Four Rock Icons Remember All Too Well."

15 Marc Spitz with Brendan Mullen, *We Got the Neutron Bomb:
    The Untold Story of L.A. Punk* (New York: Crown, 2001), 276.

16 Marc Spitz with Brendan Mullen, *We Got the Neutron Bomb:
    The Untold Story of L.A. Punk.*

17 Craig Marks, "Forty Years Ago, MTV Changed Music Forever. These Four Rock Icons Remember All Too Well."

18 Devon Ivie, "The Most Punk, Irreverent, and Joyous of the Go-Go's, According to Belinda Carlisle," *Vulture*, March 25, 2021, https://www.vulture.com/2021/03/interview-belinda -carlisle-on-the-go-gos-and-rock-hall.html.

19 Ivie, "The Most Punk, Irreverent, and Joyous of the Go-Go's, According to Belinda Carlisle."

20 Lisa A. Lewis, "Female Address on Music Television. Being Discovered," *Jump Cut: A Review of Contemporary Media*, April 1990, 2–15.

21 Lewis, "Female Address on Music Television. Being Discovered."

22 Gwen Hofmann, "Women Musicians in the 80s Used Music Videos to Expand Notions of Womanhood," *Bitch Flicks*. Accessed July 1, 2022. https://www.btchflcks.com/2016/06/ female-musicians-in-the-80s-used-music-videos-to-expand -notions-of-womanhood.html.

23 Lewis, "Female Address on Music Television. Being Discovered."

24 "Rock's New Women," *Newsweek*, March 4, 1985. Accessed June 1, 2022. https://totally80s.com/article/march-1985-cyndi-lauper -covers-newsweek-magazine-rock-and-roll-woman-power.

25 "Rock's New Women," *Newsweek*.

26 Cyndi Lauper, *Cyndi Lauper: A Memoir* (New York: Atria Books, 2017), 150.

27 "Rock's New Women," *Newsweek*.

28 Robert Sam Anson, "Birth of an MTV Nation," *Vanity Fair*, June 4, 2008, https://www.vanityfair.com/news/2000/11/ mtv200011.

29 Gillian G. Gaar, *She's a Rebel: The History of Women in Rock & Roll* (New York: Seal Press, 1992), 275.

30 NPR Staff, "The Golden Age of MTV—And Yes, There Was One," NPR, November 6, 2011, https://www.npr.org/2011/11/06/141991877/the-golden-age-of-mtv-and-yes-there-was-one.

31 NPR Staff, "The Golden Age of MTV—And Yes, There Was One."

32 Craig Marks, "Forty Years Ago, MTV Changed Music Forever. These Four Rock Icons Remember All Too Well."

Chapter 6

1 Alison Ellwood, *The Go-Go's* (SHOWTIME, 2020), 1:38.

2 Sylvie Simmons, "The Go-Go's: Ready Steady Go-Go's," *Sounds* (1980). The Go-Go's. Rock's Backpages. Accessed July 13, 2022. http://www.rocksbackpages.com/Library/Article/the-go-gos-ready-steady-go-gos.

3 Hilary Hughes, "How The Go-Go's Perfected Pop-Punk," NPR, August 5, 2020, https://www.gpb.org/news/2020/08/05/how-the-go-gos-perfected-pop-punk.

4 Keaton Bell, "How the Go-Go's Found Their Beat: An Oral History," *Vogue*, August 4, 2020, https://www.vogue.com/article/go-gos-40th-anniversary-beauty-and-the-beat-oral-history-belinda-carlisle.

5 Melissa Ruggieri, "The Go-Go's Celebrate 'Girl Power' Ahead of Rock Hall Induction: We Didn't Compromise," *USA Today*, October 26, 2021, https://www.usatoday.com/story/entertainment/music/2021/10/26/go-gos-reflect-legacy-rock

-and-roll-hall-fame-induction-foo-fighters-jay-z-carole-king
-tina-tuner/8544035002/.

6   Sara Marcus, *Girls to the Front: The True Story of the Riot Grrrl Revolution* (New York: HarperCollins, 2010), 43.

7   Marcus, *Girls to the Front: The True Story of the Riot Grrrl Revolution*.

8   Marcus, *Girls to the Front: The True Story of the Riot Grrrl Revolution*.

9   Marcus, *Girls to the Front: The True Story of the Riot Grrrl Revolution*.

10 Lisa Darms, *The Riot Grrrl Collection* (New York: Feminist Press, 2013), 11.

11 Marcus, *Girls to the Front: The True Story of the Riot Grrrl Revolution*, 169.

12 Marcus, *Girls to the Front: The True Story of the Riot Grrrl Revolution*.

13 Marcus, *Girls to the Front: The True Story of the Riot Grrrl Revolution*.

14 Marcus, *Girls to the Front: The True Story of the Riot Grrrl Revolution*.

15 Marcus, *Girls to the Front: The True Story of the Riot Grrrl Revolution*, 170.

16 Marcus, *Girls to the Front: The True Story of the Riot Grrrl Revolution*, 192.

17 Evelyn McDonnell, "The Go-Go's Gave Us the Beat and So Much More," *New York Times*, August 5, 2018, https://www.nytimes.com/2018/08/05/arts/music/why-the-go-gos-mattered-head-over-heels.html.

18 Hughes, How The Go-Go's Perfected Pop-Punk."

19 Lindsay Zoladz, "The Go-Go's Made History 38 Years Ago. There's Still More to Their Story," *New York Times*, July 29, 2020, https://www.nytimes.com/2020/07/29/arts/music/the-go-gos-documentary.html.

20 Bell, "How the Go-Go's Found Their Beat: An Oral History."

21 Jeff and Steve McDonald, "Robert Palmer is a Dick and More Gospel from The Go-Go's," *Raygun*, Issue 22.

22 Paul Elliott. "The Go-Go's: The Fab Femme Five," *Q* (2002). The Go-Go's. Rock's Backpages. Accessed July 13, 2022. http://www.rocksbackpages.com/Library/Article/the-go-gos-the-fab-femme-five.

Chapter 7

1 Sam Lansky, "In Search of the Real Nicki Minaj," *Time Magazine*, February 5, 2015, https://time.com/3696884/in-search-of-the-real-nicki-minaj/.

2 Stacy Lambe, "The Millennial 100," *Rolling Stone*, October 17, 2018, https://www.rollingstone.com/culture/culture-lists/the-millennial-100-737215/putting-the-queer-in-lgbtq-738041/.

3 El Hunt, "The Story of Britney Spears' '. . . Baby One More Time,'" *NME*, October 23, 2018, https://www.nme.com/blogs/nme-blogs/story-britney-spears-baby-one-time-2392821.

4 Stephanie Webber, "Did Pink Cringe During Christina Aguilera's AMA performance?," *Us Weekly*, November 20, 2017, https://www.usmagazine.com/celebrity-news/news/did-pink-cringe-during-christina-aguileras-amas-performance/.

5   Dee Lockett, "Stop Trying to Make Pink versus Christina Aguilera Happen (Again)," *Vulture*, November 20, 2017, https://www.vulture.com/2017/11/pink-christina-aguilera-cringe-old-feud.html.

6   Brittany Spanos, "Katy Perry Vs. Taylor Swift: Pop Stars' Beef History Explained," *Rolling Stone*, May 19, 2017, https://www.rollingstone.com/music/music-news/katy-perry-vs-taylor-swift-pop-stars-beef-history-explained-122980/.

7   Sarah Grossbart, "The Complete History of Christina Aguilera and Britney Spears' Long Running Rivalry—Including Everything You Forgot," *E! News*, May 9, 2018, https://www.eonline.com/ca/news/933844/the-complete-history-of-christina-aguilera-and-britney-spears-long-running-rivalry-including-everything-you-forgot.

8   Ed Vulliamy, "High School Vixen Cashes in on Kid Appeal," *Guardian*, October 10, 1999, https://www.theguardian.com/world/1999/oct/10/edvulliamy.theobserver.

9   *Billboard* Staff, "The Evolution of Britney Spears," *Billboard*, December 10, 2016, https://www.billboard.com/music/pop/the-evolution-of-britney-spears-7534275/.

10 Cheyenne Roundtree, "Billie Eilish, Lorde and the Push for Women Pop Stars to Constantly Reinvent Themselves," *Daily Beast*, June 13, 2021, https://www.thedailybeast.com/billie-eilish-lorde-and-the-push-for-women-pop-stars-to-constantly-reinvent-themselves.

11 Roundtree, "Billie Eilish, Lorde and the Push for Women Pop Stars to Constantly Reinvent Themselves."

12 Roundtree, "Billie Eilish, Lorde and the Push for Women Pop Stars to Constantly Reinvent Themselves."

13 GrrlBandGeek, "Courtney Love: Barbara Walters Interview 1995," December 2, 2010, YouTube, 11:38, https://www .youtube.com/watch?v=2b0jtX8YWI4.

14 GrrlBandGeek, "Courtney Love: Barbara Walters Interview 1995."

15 GrrlBandGeek, "Courtney Love: Barbara Walters Interview 1995."

16 Lana Wilson, *Miss Americana* (Netflix, 2020), 2:13.

17 Wilson, *Miss Americana*.

18 Eliana Dockterman, "Taylor Swift Calls Critics of Her Songs about Exes 'Sexist,'" *Time*, October 20, 2014, https://time.com /3524641/taylor-swift-feminism-critics-sexlst/.

19 Mark Savage, "Dua Lipa Speaks Out about Sexism in the Music Industry," *BBC*, March 29, 2018, https://www.bbc.com/ news/entertainment-arts-43584939.

20 Josh Haigh, "Lily Allen Speaks Out about Sexism in the Music Industry," *NME*, March 17, 2014, https://www.nme.com/news /music/lily-allen-67-1244885.

21 Forrest Wickman, "Why Doesn't *Pitchfork* Review Artists Like Taylor Swift (Unless They're Covered by Ryan Adams)?," *Slate*, September 25, 2015, https://slate.com/culture/2015/09/ryan -adams-1989-reviewed-by-pitchfork-why-are-taylor-swifts -albums-only-worth-reviewing-when-others-cover-them.html.

22 Bailey Calfee, "Taylor Swift Isn't Going to Answer Sexist Questions about Having Children," *Nylon*, March 28, 2019, https://www.nylon.com/taylor-swift-sexist-question-kids.

23 Lucy Mangan, "*Framing Britney Spears* Review-A Sobering Look at Sexism and Celebrity," *Guardian*, February 16, 2021, https://www.theguardian.com/tv-and-radio/2021/feb/16/

framing-britney-spears-review-a-sobering-look-at-sexism
-and-celebrity-sky-now.

24   Samantha Stark, *Framing Britney Spears* (The *New York Times*
Company, 2021), 1:14.

25   Vera Papisova, "The Haim Sisters Open Up About Their
Firsthand Experiences With Harassment and Unequal Pay,"
Teen Vogue, June 16, 2018, https://www.teenvogue.com/story/
haim-music-issue.

26   Stark, *Framing Britney Spears*.

27   Ella Alexander, "Britney Spears is an Example of Why We
Urgently Need to Protect Women's Rights," *Harper's Bazaar*,
June 24, 2021, https://www.harpersbazaar.com/uk/culture/
a36824537/britney-spears-protect-womens-rights/.

28   Lindsey Sullivan, "Lady Gaga Accepts Woman of the Year
Award at *Billboard* Women in Music: Read Her Full Speech,"
Billboard, December 18, 2015, https://www.billboard.com/
music/awards/lady-gaga-billboard-women-music-full-speech
-6813845/.

29   Joe Coscarelli, "Grammys President Faces Backlash after
Saying Women Need to 'Step Up,'" *New York Times*, January
30, 2018, https://www.nytimes.com/2018/01/30/arts/music/
grammys-step-up-neil-portnow-backlash.html.

30   Gil Kaufman, "Recording Academy CEO Neil Portnow
Responds to 'Step Up' Backlash: 'I Wasn't as Articulate as
I Should Have Been,'" *Billboard*, January 30, 2018, https://
www.billboard.com/music/awards/recording-academy-ceo
-portnow-responds-step-up-backlash-8097201/.

31   Andrea Bossi, "These Are 3 of the Biggest Drivers of Gender
Inequality in Music," *Forbes*, March 26, 2021, https://www

.forbes.com/sites/andreabossi/2021/03/26/these-are-3-of-the
-biggest-reported-drivers-of-gender-inequality-in-music/?sh
=26bc988a6290.

32 Christine Bauer and Andrés Ferraro, "Music
Recommendation Algorithms Are Unfair to Female Artists,
but We Can Change That," *The Conversation*, March 30,
2021, https://theconversation.com/music-recommendation
-algorithms-are-unfair-to-female-artists-but-we-can-change
-that-158016.

33 Anwen Crawford, "The World Needs Female Rock Critics," *New
Yorker*, May 26, 2015, https://www.newyorker.com/culture/
cultural-comment/the-world-needs-female-rock-critics.

Conclusion

1 The Go-Go's, "Rock & Roll Hall of Fame Induction," October
30, 2021, https://www.rockhall.com/inductees/go-gos?gclid
=CjwKCAiAs8acBhA1EiwAgRFdw6JtMF7flA2qILMWLqv
4q1z6A.

2 The Go-Go's, "Rock & Roll Hall of Fame Induction."

3 Drew Barrymore, "House Party," *V*, no. 75, https://www
.elliottwdavid.com/drewbarrymore.

4 The Go-Go's, "Rock & Roll Hall of Fame Induction."

5 The Go-Go's, "Rock & Roll Hall of Fame Induction."

6 The Go-Go's, "Rock & Roll Hall of Fame Induction."

7 The Go-Go's, "Rock & Roll Hall of Fame Induction."

8 Randall Roberts, "'OG Punks for the Win!,'" *Los Angeles
Times*, May 12, 2021, https://www.latimes.com/entertainment

-arts/music/story/2021-05-12/the-go-gos-rock-hall-of-fame
-induction.

9   The Go-Go's, "Rock & Roll Hall of Fame Induction."

10 Evelyn McDonnell, "It's Time for the Rock & Roll Hall of
    Fame to Address Its Gender and Racial Imbalances (Guest
    Op-Ed)," *Billboard*, November 15, 2019, https://www.billboard
    .com/music/music-news/rock-roll-hall-fame-gender-racial
    -diversity-guest-opinion-evelyn-mcdonnell-8543758/.

11 McDonnell, "It's Time for the Rock & Roll Hall of Fame to
    Address Its Gender and Racial Imbalances (Guest Op-Ed)."

12 Brittany Spanos, "Janet Jackson's Rock and Roll Hall of Fame
    Induction Speech: 'Induct More Women,'" *Rolling Stone*,
    March 29, 2019, https://www.rollingstone.com/music/
    music-news/janet-jackson-rock-and-roll-hall-of-fame-2019
    -814263/.

13 Evan Minsker, "Dave Grohl and Krist Novoselic, Talk Nirvana
    Reunion, Potential Future," *Pitchfork*, April 16, 2014, https://
    pitchfork.com/news/54808-dave-grohl-and-krist-novoselic
    -talk-nirvana-reunion-potential-future/.

14 Roberts, "'OG Punks for the Win!'"

15 Hayley Cain, "Kathy Valentine of The Go-Go's Talks
    Sisterhood, Sobriety, and the Band's Rock & Roll Hall of Fame
    Induction," *Bust*, October 29, 2021, https://bust.com/music
    /198526-kathy-valentine-of-the-go-go-s-talks-sisterhood
    -sobriety-and-the-band-s-rock-and-roll-hall-of-fame
    -induction.html.

16 Annie Zaleski, "The Go-Go's Break Out Hits, 'Rock Star'
    Poses for Long Overdue Rock Hall Induction," *Rolling Stone*,
    October 30, 2021, https://www.rollingstone.com/music/music
    -news/go-gos-rock-hall-induction-1250966/.

17 *The Drew Barrymore Show*, "Drew Barrymore Gets Emotional during Unforgettable Birthday Surprise from The Go-Go's," February 22, 2022, YouTube, 4:29, https://www.youtube.com/watch?v=e_0qHcQFFAM.

18 Paul Elliott, "The Go-Go's: The Fab Femme Five," *Q* (2002). The Go-Go's. Accessed July 13, 2022. https://www.youtube.com/watch?v=e_0qHcQFFAM. http://www.rocksbackpages.com/Library/Article/the-go-gos-the-fab-femme-five.

19 Elliott, "The Go-Go's: The Fab Femme Five."

20 Jamie Crawford, *Trainwreck: Woodstock '99* (Netflix, 2022).

21 Ann Powers, "A New Canon: In Pop Music, Women Belong at the Center of the Story," NPR, July 24, 2017, https://www.wbur.org/npr/538601651/a-new-canon-in-pop-music-women-belong-at-the-center-of-the-story.

22 Powers, "A New Canon: In Pop Music, Women Belong at the Center of the Story."

23 Melissa Ruggieri, "The Go-Go's Celebrate 'Girl Power' Ahead of Rock Hall Induction: 'We Didn't Compromise,'" *USA Today*, October 26, 2021, https://www.usatoday.com/story/entertainment/music/2021/10/26/go-gos-reflect-legacy-rock-and-roll-hall-fame-induction-foo-fighters-jay-z-carole-king-tina-tuner/8544035002/.

Bibliography

Alexander, Ella. "Britney Spears is an Example of Why We Urgently Need to Protect Women's Rights." *Harper's Bazaar*, June 24, 2021. https://www.harpersbazaar.com/uk/culture/a36824537/britney-spears-protect-womens-rights/.

Anson, Robert Sam. "Birth of an MTV Nation." *Vanity Fair*, June 4, 2008. https://www.vanityfair.com/news/2000/11/mtv200011.

Badgley, William E. *Here to Be Heard: The Story of the Slits*. Head Gear Films, 2017, 1:26.

Bag, Alice (host). "We Were There: Voices from L.A. Punk's First Wave: An Oral History." *Razorcake*, #79, April/May 2014. https://razorcake.org/we-were-there-voices-from-l-a-punks-first-wave-an-oral-history-hosted-by-alice-bag/.

Barrymore, Drew. "House Party." *V*, no. 75. https://www.elliottwdavid.com/drewbarrymore.

Barton, Geoff. "Fanny: The Untold Story of the Original Queens of Noise." *Classic Rock*, 2015. Fanny. Rock's Backpages. Accessed July 13, 2022. http://www.rocksbackpages.com/Library/Article/fanny-the-untold-story-of-the-original-queens-of-noise.

Bauer, Christine. "Music Recommendation Algorithms Are Unfair to Female Artists, but We Can Change That." *The Conversation*, March 30, 2021. https://theconversation.com/music

-recommendation-algorithms-are-unfair-to-female-artists-but
-we-can-change-that-158016.

Bell, Keaton. "How the Go-Go's Found Their Beat: An Oral
History." *Vogue*, August 4, 2020. https://www.vogue.com/article
/go-gos-40th-anniversary-beauty-and-the-beat-oral-history
-belinda-carlisle.

Benatar, Pat. *Between a Heart and a Rock Place*. New York:
HarperCollins, 2010.

Billboard Staff. "The Evolution of Britney Spears." *Billboard*,
December 10, 2016. https://www.billboard.com/music/pop/the
-evolution-of-britney-spears-7534275/.

Bossi, Andrea. "These Are 3 of the Biggest Drivers of Gender
Inequality in Music." *Forbes*, March 26, 2021. https://www
.forbes.com/sites/andreabossi/2021/03/26/these-are-3-of-the
-biggest-reported-drivers-of-gender-inequality-in-music/?sh
=26bc988a6290.

Caffey, Charlotte. "Interview by Talia Schlanger." "Q," CBC. August
24, 2020. https://www.cbc.ca/radio/q/monday-aug-24-2020
-charlotte-caffey-danny-devito-and-more-1.5695517.

Cain, Hayley. "Kathy Valentine of The Go-Go's Talks Sisterhood,
Sobriety, and the Band's Rock & Roll Hall of Fame Induction."
Bust, October 29, 2021. https://bust.com/music/198526-kathy
-valentine-of-the-go-go-s-talks-sisterhood-sobriety-and-the
-band-s-rock-and-roll-hall-of-fame-induction.html.

Calfee, Bailey. "Taylor Swift Isn't Going to Answer Sexist
Questions About Having Children." *Nylon*, March 28, 2019.
https://www.nylon.com/taylor-swift-sexist-question-kids.

Carlisle, Belinda. *Lips Unsealed*. New York: Crown Publishers, 2010.

Cherkis, Jason. "The Lost Girls." *The Huffington Post Highline*, July
2015. https://highline.huffingtonpost.com/articles/en/the-lost
-girls/.

Cohen, Jonathan. "Pat Benatar Drops 'Hit Me with Your Best Shot'
After Spate of Gun Violence." *Spin*, July 22, 2022. https://www

.spin.com/2022/07/pat-benatar-drops-hit-me-with-your-best
-shot-after-spate-of-gun-violence/.

Considine, J. D. "Go-Go's Girl Talk Is Tops." *Washington Post*, July
6, 1984. https://www.washingtonpost.com/archive/lifestyle
/1984/07/06/go-gos-girl talk-is-tops/8b8685d7-8a0e-4745
-9598-fa2f061fb8ca/.

Cooper, Mark. "The Go-Go's: I-Beam, San Francisco CA." *Record
Mirror*, 1980. The Go-Go's. Rock's Backpages. Accessed July 13,
2022. http://www.rocksbackpages.com/Library/Article/the-go
-gos-i-beam-san-francisco-ca.

Coscarelli, Joe. "Grammys President Faces Backlash After Saying
Women Need to 'Step Up.'" *New York Times*, January 30, 2018.
https://www.nytimes.com/2018/01/30/arts/music/grammys
-step-up-neil-portnow-backlash.html.

Crawford, Anwen. "The World Needs Female Rock Critics." *New
Yorker*, May 26, 2015. https://www.newyorker.com/culture/
cultural-comment/the-world-needs-female-rock-critics.

Crawford, Jamie. *Trainwreck: Woodstock '99*. Netflix, 2022.

Currie, Cherie. *Neon Angel: A Memoir of a Runaway*. New York:
HarperCollins, 2010.

Darms, Lisa. *The Riot Grrrl Collection*. New York: Feminist Press,
2013.

Dockterman, Eliana. "Taylor Swift Calls Critics of Her Songs
about Exes 'Sexist.'" *Time*, October 20, 2014. https://time.com
/3524641/taylor-swift-feminism-critics-sexist/.

Elliott, Paul. "The Go-Go's: The Fab Femme Five." *Q*, 2002. The
Go-Go's. Rock's Backpages. Accessed July 13, 2022. http://
www.rocksbackpages.com/Library/Article/the-go-gos-the-fab
-femme-five.

Ellwood, Alison. *The Go-Go's*. SHOWTIME, 2020, 1:38.

Ferraro, Andrés. "Music Recommendation Algorithms Are Unfair
to Female Artists, but We Can Change That." *The Conversation*,
March 30, 2021. https://theconversation.com/music

-recommendation-algorithms-are-unfair-to-female-artists-but
-we-can-change-that-158016.

Gaar, Gillian G. *She's A Rebel: The History of Women in Rock & Roll*. New York: Seal Press, 1992.

Gaar, Gillian G. "80s Darlings The Go-Go's Prove They've Still Got the Beat." *Goldmine*, November 28, 2011. https://www .goldminemag.com/articles/80s-darlings-the-go-gos-prove -theyve-still-got-the-beat.

Gevinson, Tavi. "Britney Spears Was Never in Control." *The Cut*, February 23, 2021. https://www.thecut.com/2021/02/tavi -gevinson-britney-spears-was-never-in-control.html.

GrrlBandGeek. "Courtney Love: Barbara Walters Interview 1995," December 2, 2010, YouTube, 11:38, https://www.youtube.com/ watch?v=2b0jtX8YWI4.

Go-Go's, The. *Behind the Music*. YouTube, 43:19, April 23, 2018.

Go-Go's, The. "Bio." Accessed June 10, 2022. https://www.gogos .com/bio/.

Go-Go's, The. "Rock & Roll Hall of Fame Induction." October 30, 2021. https://www.rockhall.com/inductees/go-gos?gclid =CjwKCAiAs8acBhA1EiwAgRFdw6JtMF7flA2qILMWLqv 4q1z6A.

Golden, Audrey. "The Go-Go's Beauty and the Beat: A 40th Anniversary Celebration." *Louder Than War*, July 8, 2021. https://louderthanwar.com/the-go-gos-beauty-and-the-beat-a -40th-anniversary-celebration/.

Goldstein, Toby. "The Go-Go's: *Beauty and the Beat* (IRS)." *Musician*, 1981. The Go-Go's. Rock's Backpages. Accessed August 1, 2022. http://www.rocksbackpages.com/Library/ Article/the-go-gos-ibeauty-and-the-beati-irs.

Grossbart, Sarah. "The Complete History of Christina Aguilera and Britney Spears' Long Running Rivalry—Including Everything You Forgot." *E! News*, May 9, 2018. https://www .eonline.com/ca/news/933844/the-complete-history-of

-christina-aguilera-and-britney-spears-long-running-rivalry
-including-everything-you-forgot.

Haigh, Josh. "Lily Allen Speaks Out About Sexism in the Music Industry." *NME*, March 17, 2014. https://www.nme.com/news/music/lily-allen-67-1244885.

Harrington, Richard. "The Go-Go's Go Get 'Em." *The Washington Post*, September 19, 1982. https://www.washingtonpost.com/archive/lifestyle/style/1982/09/19/the-go-gos-go-get-em/46b2f76b-aa0c-4549-a70e-f266a451180f/.

Harris, Misty. "Female Artists 'Hypersexualized' by Rolling Stone: Study." *Windsor Star*, July 26, 2011. https://windsorstar.com/news/female-artists-hypersexualized-by-rolling-stone-study.

Harry, Debbie. *Face It*. New York: Dey Street Books, 2019.

Hirshey, Gerri. *We Gotta Get Out of This Place: The True, Tough Story of Women in Rock*. New York: Grove Press, 2002.

Hofmann, Gwen. "Women Musicians in the 80s Used Music Videos to Expand Notions of Womanhood." *Bitch Flicks*, https://www.btchflcks.com/2016/06/female-musicians-in-the-80s-used-music-videos-to-expand-notions-of-womanhood.html. Accessed July 1, 2022.

Hopper, Jessica. "'It Was Us Against Those Guys': The Women Who Transformed *Rolling Stone* in the Mid-70s." *Vanity Fair*, August 28, 2018. https://www.vanityfair.com/style/2018/08/the-women-who-transformed-rolling-stone-in-the-mid-70s.

Hughes, Hilary. "How The Go-Go's Perfected Pop-Punk." NPR, August 5, 2020. https://www.gpb.org/news/2020/08/05/how-the-go-gos-perfected-pop-punk.

Hunt, El Hunt. "The Story of Britney Spears' '. . . Baby One More Time.'" *NME*, October 23, 2018. https://www.nme.com/blogs/nme-blogs/story-britney-spears-baby-one-time-2392821.

Ivie, Devon. "The Most Punk, Irreverent, and Joyous of the Go-Go's, According to Belinda Carlisle." *Vulture*, March 25, 2021.

https://www.vulture.com/2021/03/interview-belinda-carlisle
-on-the-go-gos-and-rock-hall.html.

Johnson, Kathleen. "Fanny's June Millington: Grrrl Power's First
Flash in Rock." *Vintage Guitar*. https://www.vintageguitar.com
/27947/fannys-june-millington/. Accessed August 1, 2022.

Johnson, Rick. "The Runaways." *Creem*, April 1977.

Jones, Rhian E. "Post-Punk: Raw, Female Sound," in *Women
Make Noise: Girl Bands from Motown to the Modern*, ed. Julia
Downes. Twickenham: Supernova Books, 2012.

Kapadia, Asif. *Amy*. James Gay-Rees, 2015, 2:16.

Kaufman, Gil. "Recording Academy CEO Neil Portnow Responds
to 'Step Up' Backlash: 'I Wasn't as Articulate as I should Have
Been.'" *Billboard*, January 30, 2018. https://www.billboard.com/
music/awards/recording-academy-ceo-portnow-responds-step
-up-backlash-8097201/.

Lambe, Stacy. "The Millennial 100." *Rolling Stone*, October 17,
2018. https://www.rollingstone.com/culture/culture-lists
/the-millennial-100-737215/putting-the-queer-in-lgbtq
-738041/.

Lansky, Sam. "In Search of the Real Nicki Minaj." *Time Magazine*,
February 5, 2015. https://time.com/3696884/in-search-of-the
-real-nicki-minaj/.

Lauper, Cyndi. *Cyndi Lauper: A Memoir*, 150. New York: Atria
Books, 2017.

Lewis, Lisa A. "Female Address on Music Television. Being
Discovered." *Jump Cut: A Review of Contemporary Media*, April
1990.

Lockett, Dee. "Stop Trying to Make Pink Versus Christina Aguilera
Happen (Again)." *Vulture*, November 20, 2017. https://www
.vulture.com/2017/11/pink-christina-aguilera-cringe-old-feud
.html.

Lupo, Jane. "Go-Go's." *Trouser Press*, 1981. https://www.gogos.com
/2011/06/25/from-the-vault-trouser-press-1981/.

Majewksi, Lori and Jonathan Bernstein. *Mad World: An Oral History of New Wave Artists and Songs That Defined the 1980s.* New York: Abrams, 2014.

Mangan, Lucy. "*Framing Britney Spears* Review-A Sobering Look at Sexism and Celebrity." *Guardian*, February 16, 2021. https://www.theguardian.com/tv-and-radio/2021/feb/16/framing-britney-spears-review-a-sobering-look-at-sexism-and-celebrity-sky-now.

Marcus, Sara. *Girls to the Front: The True Story of the Riot Grrrl Revolution.* New York: HarperCollins, 2010.

Marks, Craig. "Forty Years Ago, MTV Changed Music Forever. These Four Rock Icons Remember All Too Well." *Los Angeles Times*, July 28, 2021. https://www.latimes.com/entertainment-arts/music/story/2021-07-28/mtv-40th-anniversary-billy-idol-go-gos-huey-lewis-reo-speedwagon.

McDonald, Steve and Jeff McDonald. "Robert Palmer is a Dick and More Gospel From the Go-Go's." *Raygun*, Issue 22.

McDonnell, Evelyn. "The Go-Go's Gave Us the Beat and So Much More." *New York Times*, August 5, 2018. https://www.nytimes.com/2018/08/05/arts/music/why-the-go-gos-mattered-head-over-heels.html.

McDonnell, Evelyn. "It's Time for the Rock & Roll Hall of Fame to Address Its Gender and Racial Imbalances (Guest Op-Ed)." *Billboard*, November 15, 2019. https://www.billboard.com/music/music-news/rock-roll-hall-fame-gender-racial-diversity-guest-opinion-evelyn-mcdonnell-8543758/.

Minsker, Evan. "Dave Grohl and Krist Novoselic, Talk Nirvana Reunion, Potential Future." *Pitchfork*, April 16, 2014. https://pitchfork.com/news/54808-dave-grohl-and-krist-novoselic-talk-nirvana-reunion-potential-future/.

Moore, Tracy. "There's More to *The Go-Go's* Than Peppy Hits." *Vanity Fair*, August 3, 2020. https://www.vanityfair.com/hollywood/2020/08/the-go-gos-documentary-music-showtime.

Moreland, Quinn. "Beauty and the Beat: The Go-Go's." *Pitchfork*, October 20, 2019. https://pitchfork.com/reviews/albums/the-go-gos-beauty-and-the-beat/.

Newsweek, Staff. "Rock's New Women." *Newsweek*, March 4, 1985. https://totally80s.com/article/march-1985-cyndi-lauper-covers-newsweek-magazine-rock-and-roll-woman-power. (Accessed June 1, 2022).

NPR, Staff. "The Golden Age of MTV—And Yes, There Was One." NPR, November 6, 2011. https://www.npr.org/2011/11/06/141991877/the-golden-age-of-mtv-and-yes-there-was-one.

Oksanen, Atte. "Female Rock Stars and Addiction in Autobiographies." *Nordic Studies on Alcohol and Drugs* 30 (November 2012). https://journals.sagepub.com/doi/pdf/10.2478/nsad-2013-0009.

Panebianco, Julie. "Hey Hey! We're the Go-Go's!," *Boston Rock*, 1981. The Go-Go's, The Specials. Rock's Backpages. Accessed August 2, 2022. http://www.rocksbackpages.com/Library/Article/hey-hey-were-the-go-gos.

Papisova, Vera. "The Haim Sisters Open Up About Their Firsthand Experiences With Harassment and Unequal Pay." *Teen Vogue*, June 16, 2018. https://www.teenvogue.com/story/haim-music-issue.

Parker, Lyndsey. "The Go-Go's Talk Partying Past, Hall of Fame Snub and 'Emotional' Documentary." *Yahoo Music*, July 29, 2020. https://ca.sports.yahoo.com/news/the-go-gos-talk-partying-past-hall-of-fame-snub-and-emotional-documentary-you-cant-deny-what-weve-done-221531086.html.

People Magazine, Staff. 1981. https://www.gogos.com/2011/05/17/from-the-vault-people-magazine/.

Pond, Steve. "The Go-Go's: Ladies First." *Rolling Stone*, August 5, 1982. https://www.rollingstone.com/music/music-news/the-go-gos-ladies-first-89680/.

Powers, Ann. "A New Cannon: In Pop Music, Women Belong at the Center of the Story." NPR, July 24, 2017. https://www.wbur.org/npr/538601651/a-new-canon-in-pop-music-women-belong-at-the-center-of-the-story.

Roberts, Randall. "'OG Punks for the Win!'" *Los Angeles Times*, May 12, 2021. https://www.latimes.com/entertainment-arts/music/story/2021-05-12/the-go-gos-rock-hall-of-fame-induction.

Roundtree, Cheyenne. "Billie Eilish, Lorde and the Push for Women Pop Stars to Constantly Reinvent Themselves." *Daily Beast*, June 13, 2021. https://www.thedailybeast.com/billie-eilish-lorde-and-the-push-for-women-pop-stars-to-constantly-reinvent-themselves.

Ruggieri, Melissa. "The Go-Go's Celebrate 'Girl Power' Ahead of Rock Hall Induction: We Didn't Compromise." *USA Today*, October 26, 2021. https://www.usatoday.com/story/entertainment/music/2021/10/26/go-gos-reflect-legacy-rock-and-roll-hall-fame-induction-foo-fighters-jay-z-carole-king-tina-tuner/8544035002/.

Sankey, Elizabeth. "From Punk Rock to Sugar Pop: Tracing the Music and Style of the Go-Go's." *Vice*, September 23, 2014. https://www.vice.com/en/article/ryy9kr/from-punk-rock-to-sugar-pop-tracing-the-music-and-style-of-the-go-gos.

Savage, Mark. "Dua Lipa Speaks Out about Sexism in the Music Industry." *BBC*, March 29, 2018. https://www.bbc.com/news/entertainment-arts-43584939.

Simmons, Sylvie. "The Go-Go's: Ready Steady Go-Go's." *Sounds*, 1980. The Go-Go's. Rock's Backpages. Accessed August 15, 2022. http://www.rocksbackpages.com/Library/Article/the-go-gos-ready-steady-go-gos.

Slash Magazine. September 1978.

Slash Magazine. January 1979.

Slash Magazine. Vol 3. No. 5.

Snowden, Don. "The Go-Gos Go!!" *New York Rocker*, 1980. The Go-Go's. Rock's Backpages. Accessed July 13, 2022. http://www .rocksbackpages.com/Library/Article/the-go-gos-go.

Spanos, Brittany. "Katy Perry Vs. Taylor Swift: Pop Stars' Beef History Explained." *Rolling Stone*, May 19, 2017. https://www .rollingstone.com/music/music-news/katy-perry-vs-taylor -swift-pop-stars-beef-history-explained-122980/.

Spanos, Brittany. "Janet Jackson's Rock and Roll Hall of Fame Induction Speech: 'Induct More Women.'" *Rolling Stone*, March 29, 2019. https://www.rollingstone.com/music/music-news/ janet-jackson-rock-and-roll-hall-of-fame-2019-814263/.

Spitz, Marc with Brendan Mullen. *We Got the Neutron Bomb: The Untold Story of L.A. Punk*. New York: Crown, 2001.

Stand, Mike. "Go-Go's." *Smash Hits*, 1982. The Go-Go's. Rock's Backpages. Accessed August 15, 2022. http://www .rocksbackpages.com/Library/Article/go-gos.

Stark, Samantha. *Framing Britney Spears*. The New York Times Company, 2021, 1:14.

Stricklin, Sandra L. "The Fine Art of Fun—A Big Part of the Go-Go's Success Story." *The Christian Science Monitor*, May 18, 1982. https://www.csmonitor.com/layout/set/amphtml/1982 /0518/051801.html.

Sullivan, Lindsey. "Lady Gaga Accepts Woman of the Year Award at *Billboard* Women in Music: Read Her Full Speech." *Billboard*, December 18, 2015. https://www.billboard.com/music/awards/ lady-gaga-billboard-women-music-full-speech-6813845/.

Tannenbaum, Rob. "The Go-Go's Recall the Debauched Days of Their Hit 'We Got the Beat' 35 Years Later." *Billboard*, May 20, 2016. https://www.billboard.com/music/pop/the-go-gos-we -got-the-beat-35th-anniversary-interview-billboard-music -awards-7378161/.

The Drew Barrymore Show. "Drew Barrymore Gets Emotional During Unforgettable Birthday Surprise from The Go-Go's."

February 22, 2022, YouTube, 4:29, https://www.youtube.com/watch?v=e_0qHcQFFAM.

Valentine, Kathy. *All I Ever Wanted*. Austin: University of Texas Press, 2020.

Vulliamy, Ed. "High School Vixen Cashes in on Kid Appeal." *Guardian*, October 10, 1999. https://www.theguardian.com/world/1999/oct/10/edvulliamy.theobserver.

Walters, John. "How the Retiring Go-Go's became the Ideal Soundtrack to Suburban Teen Rebellion." *Newsweek*, August 30, 2016. https://www.newsweek.com/go-gos-play-their-final-show-l-tracing-how-they-became-ideal-soundtrack-494589.

Webber, Stephanie. "Did Pink Cringe during Christina Aguilera's AMA Performance?" *Us Weekly*, November 20, 2017. https://www.usmagazine.com/celebrity-news/news/did-pink-cringe-during-christina-aguileras-amas-performance/.

Wickman, Forrest. "Why Doesn't *Pitchfork* Review Artists Like Taylor Swift (Unless They're Covered by Ryan Adams)?" *Slate*, September 25, 2015. https://slate.com/culture/2015/09/ryan-adams-1989-reviewed-by-pitchfork-why-are-taylor-swifts-albums-only-worth-reviewing-when-others-cover-them.html.

Wilson, Lana. *Miss Americana*. Netflix, 2020, 2:13.

Wiser, Carl Wiser. "Jane Wiedlin of the Go-Go's." *Songfacts*, 2007. The Go-Go's, Jane Wiedlin. Rock's Backpages. Accessed July 13, 2022. http://www.rocksbackpages.com/Library/Article/jane-wiedlin-of-the-go-gos.

Zaleski, Annie. "The Go-Go's Break Out Hits, 'Rock Star' Poses for Long Overdue Rock Hall Induction." *Rolling Stone*, October 30, 2021. https://www.rollingstone.com/music/music-news/go-gos-rock-hall-induction-1250966/.

Zoladz, Lindsay. "The Go-Go's Made History 38 Years Ago. There's Still More to Their Story." *New York Times*, July 29, 2020. https://www.nytimes.com/2020/07/29/arts/music/the-go-gos-documentary.html.

Also available in the series

ALSO AVAILABLE IN THE SERIES

ALSO AVAILABLE IN THE SERIES